SPAIN

Fray Luis de Granada

TWAS 438

Fray Luis de Granada

FRAY LUIS
DE GRANADA

By JOHN A. MOORE
College of William and Mary

TWAYNE PUBLISHERS
A DIVISION OF G. K. HALL & CO., BOSTON

Library of Congress Cataloging in Publication Data

Moore, John Aiken, 1920–
   Fray Luis de Granada.

   (Twayne's world authors series ; TWAS 438 : Spain)
   Bibliography: p. 157–58.
   Includes index.
   1. Luis de Granada, 1504–1588.   2. Authors, Spanish—
16th century—Biography.
PQ6412.L8Z75   271'.2'024   76-55365
ISBN 0-8057-6276-0

Contents

About the Author

John A. Moore was born in Badin, N. C. in 1920. He received his B.S. degree from Davidson College 1942, his M.A. in 1948 and his Ph. D. in 1954, both from the University of North Carolina. He also attended the University of the Americas in Mexico and the Universities of Cartagena and of the Andes in Colombia. He served in the U. S. Army Air Force 1942–6. Since 1950 he has been teaching at the College of William and Mary, becoming full Professor in 1965.

Dr. Moore was a member of the first Fulbright program for teachers in Colombia in 1958 and a fellow of the Southeastern Institute for Medieval and Renaissance Studies at Duke University in 1966. Also he was a member of the Danforth Workshop in Liberal Arts, Colorado College, 1963.

He is a member of the American Association of Teachers of Spanish and Portuguese (AATSP) and the South Atlantic Modern Language Association (SAMLA). He has served on SAMLA's Executive Committee. He is a former member of the Modern Language Association and the American Association of University Professors, having served as Chapter President and representative to the National Convention. He is the author of a TWAS volume on *Ramón de la Cruz* and of a number of articles on Spanish literary topics published in *Hispania, Romance Notes* and the *South Atlantic Bulletin*, and has completed indexes for *Hispania* and for *Romance Notes*.

Preface

This analysis of Granada which arose out of my doctoral dissertation, is largely my own, partly because scholars of today do not often make contributions to Granadan studies. There is a chapter on the critics, but as the reader can easily observe, the chapter is thin. With one cited exception the few translations from the Spanish or French included in this book are mine.

Granada has many homely virtues which present something of a problem in a treatment of his work: to discuss them with the matter-of-fact tone that insures objectivity may also guarantee tedium; while to present them so as to recapture Granada's own enthusiasm risks banality. Nevertheless, the patient reader should find that the study of Fray Luis's work is ultimately rewarding. One discovers that Granada's austerity is not fanaticism; his humility is evidence neither of a lack of confidence nor of inverted pride. His love of God is not expressed as a compensation for his inability to face the world. Granada wrote to place the erudition of the scholar at the command of the average Christian. I hope that the description of this process will be of interest to the scholarly.

Granada was prolific, and this book represents a study of all of his major Castilian works, in addition to a sampling of Latin works in Spanish translation. Since Granada himself stated that the material of all of his works is contained in the ones treated here, I do not think that this volume could be essentially improved by dealing with his additional writings.

I am indebted to Professors James C. Livingston and Alexander Kurtz of the William and Mary Faculty for assistance with theological problems. The former assisted me during the initial phase while the latter read the manuscript and saved me from some *faux pas.* Any remaining misinterpretations must be attributed to the imperfections of this author in carrying out their advice.

My conviction is that Granada and his works merit an honored place in the *Twayne World Authors Series,* and I am hopeful that this volume fulfills the need.

JOHN A. MOORE

College of William and Mary

Chronology

1582   Granada publishes first four volumes of *Introduction to the Symbol of Faith (Introducción al símbolo de la fe)*.

1585   Granada publishes fifth volume of *Introduction to the Symbol of Faith (Introducción al símbolo de la fe)*.

1588   December 31, Granada dies in Lisbon.

CHAPTER 1

Introduction: The Religious Scene

I *The Religious Crisis in the Time of Granada*

IT is my intention in this introduction to set a tone for the book and to stress a personal attitude which will serve as a frame of reference for remarks elsewhere. In situations where one person's dogma is another person's heresy or superstition, it is well to emphasize that the attitudes expressed here are not to be considered as authoritative pronouncements but rather as personal interpretations. Fortunately, Granada himself steered clear of religious controversies which he felt were not of concern to his readers. Therefore, I intend generally to avoid issues not relevant to understanding Fray Luis and hope that the reader can forgive me when my interpretations reveal that I am merely a Protestant layman.

It will be helpful at least to sketch the broadest outlines of sixteenth-century religious controversy. Fray Luis de Granada was twenty-one years younger than Martin Luther and some thirty-eight years younger than Erasmus. He was too young to have influenced the immediate reaction to Luther's Wittenberg theses or to the Diet of Worms.[1] He followed with interest the developments of at least a part of the Council of Trent, since his good friend Fray Bartolomé de los Mártires, Archbishop of Braga took an active role there, and Granada was to become his biographer. Since Granada never left the Iberian peninsula, he was far from the front lines of the original Protestant-Catholic confrontation. He was never directly involved in the formulation of the official Church attitudes toward controversial matters. Nevertheless, he certainly felt the influence of these events, however remotely, and therefore we should deal, at least briefly with some of the principles.

The Protestants declined to unite under one theological banner or one organization, and there was, therefore, no monolithic Protestant view which could be contrasted with the Catholic position. On the other hand, Granada's concern with the Protestants never reached the point of his analyzing Protestant theology on any issue; therefore, as far as he was concerned, the movement presumably seemed monolithic. He seldom referred to Protestants except for allegations of persecutions of some Catholics in Elizabethan England. He undoubtedly did include them under the name "heretics" from time to time. From his writings we must assume that he considered Protestants wicked men first and heretics second.

The Catholic Church has long maintained that it is the authentic intermediary between an individual and God. It believes that it has been given a revealed Truth and that it has been charged with interpreting this unchanging basic Truth in a changing world. If Catholics believe firmly that Christ, through His Vicar, St. Peter, established the church as His one official liaison to man, why should any man seek an alternative way of communing with Him? The church has sacraments which it holds to be divinely ordained to give men special help at significant points in their lives, providing for man's salvation and his maintenance in a state of Grace.

The catalyst for the break with Luther was the difference of attitude toward indulgences. The concept of indulgences was practical. If a man wished to atone for his sins, he could perform acts pleasing to God and showing evidence of his contrition, while having the church supervise these acts gave a reassuring authenticity to the repentant sinner. Theologically this practice was atonement, not salvation, though one might assume that this distinction could have been misunderstood by many laymen and even priests.

Luther's theological banner read, "justification by grace through faith alone." Although St. James was not Luther's favorite letter writer, he knew that in his epistle St. James had said that "faith without works is dead." If faith has any meaning, it will inspire a person to conduct himself in accordance with the mandates of his faith and thus imply the performance of good works. It was important to Luther, however, that faith be considered basic and that good works be held to be derivative. The practice of indulgences meant that a person would be in part earning his own atonement, and frequently by agreements which were as convenient to the church materially as they were helpful to the individual spiritually. For many of the reformers "works" came to mean principally the rites, rituals, and official pronouncements of the church. Many good Catholics, including Granada, recognized the corruption exemplified and symbolized by the abuse of the indulgences, but still maintained that the church functions themselves were divinely established for man's spiritual help. The church was God's surrogate with complete authority. The application of Luther's doctrine could short-circuit all of the good offices of the church by reducing or eliminating that authority. The church would not sanction compromise with Luther, as his friend Melanchthon sadly learned.[2]

Despite the furor over Luther, Erasmus was the greater menace to orthodoxy for the conservative, sixteenth-century Spaniard.[3] For Erasmus it was the interpretation of St. Paul rather than the primacy of St. Peter that was central to the church's problem. For St. Paul, the big question was faith versus the law, that is, the Mosaic law elaborately developed by the Pharisees. St. Paul, who was himself a Pharisee, did not repudiate the law but maintained that it had been superseded by the coming of Christ. The danger of dependence upon the law was that it could become interpreted so literally that it bound one's spirit and induced self-righteousness. Our usual picture today of a Pharisee is one who observes rites mechanically and thinks he is fulfilling his duty. Erasmus felt that the dogma of the church was being allowed to be interpreted in the same manner to resemble the spiritual emptiness exemplified by the name Pharisee. Erasmus criticized the operations of the church but would not reject the church nor would he allow himself to be pushed out.

The extent to which Erasmus's reforms were necessary need not concern us here. The point is that many Spanish religious leaders thought that he was dangerously wrong. While the church in Spain remained united as an institution, it maintained a struggle between the Erasmian and conservative points of view within the church which was strong enough to keep the Inquisition busy and to spawn considerable religious persecution. The internal threat thus seemed greater to conservative religious authorities than did the external menace of Protestantism. In fact, some felt that the two were related.

The Inquisition's function was not to fight against immorality but against heresy. Since it was concerned about those people who, according to the Inquisition's standards, were worshipping the wrong way, and especially those who were teaching others an unorthodox approach to worship, it often persecuted or restricted people who, from our twentieth-century point of view, were among the most fervent servants of God. Anyone of conspicuous piety might become suspect. One may suggest that a person in almost any age is in greater danger within his own society for expressing his religion too zealously than for failure to express his religion at all. Furthermore, anyone deeply absorbed in his religious fervor might be oblivious to the concern he was causing the public and not alert to the precautions needed to remain acceptable in the eyes of Inquisitors.

In the early sixteenth century a number of religious Spaniards seeking a personal religious experience through mental prayer and other spiritual exercises became suspect in the eyes of the rigidly orthodox. They soon acquired labels such as *alumbrado, iluminado* ("enlightened") or *dejado* ("passivist").[4] The first stage *recogido* ("recollected") was an accepted stage which meant simply that for proper observance of religious duties there was an effort to concentrate attention upon spiritual matters. Its purpose was to enhance the meaning of the rituals. If these experiences seemed to become meaningful in themselves, replacing the formal ritual and giving the idea that the individual could find God without the direct influence of the Church, he was considered *alumbrado* ("enlightened"). A few interpreted their spiritual exercises as the attainment of immunity to the normal requirements of morality. Their action cast suspicion upon all who used meditation and contemplation, especially those not members of a monastic order. There is a similarity, usually superficial, between these religious exercises and those of the great mystics, but mystics themselves are among the most chary of believing that they have had rare religious experiences and they remain constantly on the alert to distinguish between the true mystical experience and misleading experiences superficially similar to the mystical.[5]

The movement that inspired the name *alumbrado* was not often represented by extremists, who rightly could concern the Inquisition. It was very likely that a genuine mystic could be thought of as an *alumbrado*. If the reader will for the moment imagine himself as a sixteenth-century Spanish Catholic trying to become informed about Protestants, *alumbrados*, and other "heretics," he will understand this suspicion of spiritual exercises in which a person seeks a direct communion with Christ. He is told what an *alumbrado* is and how he gets that way. The approach of the Pharisee seems much safer.

The movement against the *alumbrados* ("enlightened ones") began to gather momentum under Charles V but intensified during the reign of Philip II. The conservative church leader Melchor Cano and the Inquisitor General Fernando Valdés were now ready to move against the preaching and publishing of exercises reminding them of the *alumbrados*. Most of those alleged to be *alumbrados* continued to participate in regular church Sacraments and other functions, but this demonstration of orthodox activity was not always a guarantee of inquisitorial restraint. The first major *Index* of prohibited books in Spain came out in 1559. In many cases the inquisitor's verdict was simply the requirement of revising a book to remove matter which the inquisitor felt could lead to an unorthodox line of thinking. The leading religious writers of the sixteenth century in Spain (Luis de Granada, Luis de León, St. Theresa, and St. John of the Cross) all felt, in varying degrees, the restraining force of those who believed that they were thus protecting the purity of the faith and the welfare of the church.

Central to the *alumbrado* controversy is the question of mental prayer. When a person prays, he normally either recites a prayer which he has learned or else expresses his thoughts to God in his own words. Obviously, anyone can pray in this manner if he cares to. Mental prayer is done without words and is far more difficult, since it requires greater concentration upon the prayer. A person may make a brief mental prayer unconsciously if a child steps off a curb with a truck approaching, but a conscious and sustained mental prayer is different. Its purpose is less to talk than to listen. It is considered by most mystics to be an introduction to the state of mind needed to be receptive to mystical states.

It should not surprise us that sharp differences of opinion could arise over the universal acceptance of mental prayer. If a man or woman seeks spiritual comforts through mental prayer he or she might easily imagine hearing the voice of God. The wish could easily substitute for the experience. If the person then seeks to report the imagined experience as fact, the church authorities become concerned. Therefore, if a man such as Granada writes a book in which mental prayer is advocated for every Christian, a conservative censor like Valdés would see danger in having it read. Granada himself was a liberal with respect to mental prayer. He seems not to have seen danger in any form of prayer.

II *The Nature of Religious Practice*

Meanwhile, in monastery, convent, or wherever humble Spanish men and women tried to consecrate their lives to Christ, life was only tangentially affected by the theological controversy dividing religious experts. There were two principal ways of serving Christ, often designated as the way of Martha and the way of Mary. Martha believed in doing humble practical chores, but her sister, Mary, who had a flair for the dramatic, poured ointment on Christ's head (Matthew 26 and John 12). When she was rebuked for her extravagance, Jesus defended her, saying that her act was prophetic preparation for his burial. In time, Mary became symbolic for Christians of the mystical approach to religious activity as did Martha of the practical or by extension, the ascetic approach.

Most religious writers were a combination of the two, though some may have stressed one approach far more than the other. Many people sought the ascetic life because they looked upon the world as generally wicked. If a person believed that his body was moved by worldly impulses and sought to suppress them, he did not try to curb his passions in a spirit of moderation; instead, he sought to stifle them completely, substituting any practice which would occupy his time, provide a stimulus for his mind, and fill, with whatever he considered useful and pious, the vacuum left by elimination of the worldly impulse. These occupations usually meant menial work, study, and prayer. The enemies were not only the deadly sins but also those activities which today are considered normal, such as sleeping, eating, and informal conversations, all of which should be reduced, according to ascetic standards, to the minimum. One reason for living in a monastery was to get help from others in this rigorously disciplined life. Living there was learning to endure hardships, punishing the body with hair shirts or self-flagellation, knowing that with the help of God and of the brothers, one would eventually mortify the flesh and purify the soul.

The body's physical activities were to be controlled by the will. Thus mental discipline was more important than physical. If one spent most of his day thinking of how evil his body was, how important it was to get it under control so that the spirit could command, and what a contrast there was between worldly evil and God's mercy, the mind would gradually become disciplined enough to drive out, sublimate, or otherwise control the animal instincts. A book such as the *Contemptus mundi,* attributed to Thomas à Kempis, usually translated into English with the title *The Imitation of Christ,* was a strong support for anyone seeking an ascetic existence. Granada's first literary work was a translation of the *Contemptus mundi* into Spanish.

One would think that such people would "psych" themselves into severe mental health problems, and some undoubtedly did. Satan would get the credit for that. Apparently most were able to lead normal (by psychological definition) lives, their libidos finding ways of expression and release, sustained by an inner peace and the monastic discipline.

Not all ascetics approached life as a fearful struggle against sin. For some, austerity was natural, so their's was a positive approach rather than the negative goal of simply avoiding occasions for sinning. And of course, not all of those who took vows held such single-minded dedication to this concept of virtue. A large part of St. Theresa's time and energy was spent in a reform movement for her order that took much of her amazing energy. She constantly fought the passive resistance that every zealot encounters from those less strongly motivated, but she also encountered active opposition from those with fundamental objections to her way of life and her ideas for its implementation. If all monasteries and convents were filled with those who zealously maintained the ascetic standards, presumably there would have been no need for Fray Luis de Granada to write his books. These works did, however, assume that the ascetic life was the ideal toward which the monk or nun should strive, and were written to help the average person to live up to this ideal.

The ascetic way did not threaten the church's control over the mind of man. The mystical way, however, was at least partly beyond the church's control. It represented direct communion of the soul with God as revealed in ways different in nature and degree from His normal revelation of His presence to all men. The idea that God should give a special comfort to the person who deserved it or needed it seemed to fit well into the general idea that the sixteenth century held of His nature. If a person believed that God had come to him in a special way, should he tell his brother? Should he go further and tell him how it happened? The church recognizes the principle that God chooses to reveal His presence to a few in a special way to inspire them so that they may guide and inspire others, but the church is reluctant to accept too readily specific claims of mystical experience. The mystic may find the normal channels of living inadequate to express the love stored within him; that love which finds its fulfillment in the mystic way. On the other hand, if a person finds that he is inadequate to face the world, would he not be tempted to imagine mystical experiences that he could tell to impress his brothers? How does the outsider distinguish between the true and the imagined? Can an individual always recognize the reality of mystical experience? The raising of these questions indicates that the church leaders could and indeed sometimes did differ among themselves in their attitudes toward mystical experiences and spiritual exercises.

A person probably should make his own definition of mysticism inductively after becoming acquainted with numerous examples of its operation, but for convenience I cite here a definition quoted by Evelyn Underhill: "Mysticism is the concentration of all the forces of the soul upon a supernatural object, conceived and loved as a living Person."[6] This definition should be acceptable to the skeptic, who presumably can accept the fact that people of different religions, in different ages, and with no possible contact with one another, have manifested similar experiences that simply cannot be dismissed as pious illusions, whatever their logical explanation may be. Many strive through contemplation to become mystics. A few do become mystics in this way, and a still smaller number have mystical experiences without seeking them. A working definition of mysticism can be so strict as to accept as mystics only the most conspicuous and complete examples, or it can be considered very broadly to include anyone who sincerely and persistently practices contemplation. If one considers mysticism broadly, mystics may differ from ordinary people only in the degree of their dedication to the mystic way. If one considers it narrowly, the mystic is one whose contemplations have taken him so far from ordinary thoughts that he has apparently entered a realm of experience utterly beyond the experiences of mankind in general. He has enjoyed ineffable delights which he can recount only in highly symbolic language and then only with a feeling that any metaphor is inadequate fully to explain. Many others have a less vivid awareness of the Supernatural presence, but their limited experience may serve to corroborate the testimony of the great mystics. This seems true because the lesser mystics' experiences seem like stages in the development of that of the greater ones.

The mystical response was quite different from the ascetic's although not necessarily antithetical to it. Primarily, the mystic was the lover, rather than the servant, of God. Some men and women were both ascetic and mystic, at one time the servant, at another the lover. The mystic *qua* mystic did not mortify the flesh and try to exorcize the evil within him. The mystic would meditate upon some aspect of God's love or perhaps upon God's existence or presence and soon transcend any guilt feelings which his ascetic nature was struggling against. The mystic's will takes on an ambivalent quality, since it must be actively driving the soul to a close concentration upon its meditations, yet be passively free to be led by the unseen Power. With successful experience the soul learns how to abandon itself to the Divine Will without losing the conscious drive to remove all distracting influence.

The Spanish mystics did have a quality that distinguished them (and other European mystics) from some Eastern mystics. The Spanish mystic never lost consciousness of his identity as an individual. He did not experience nirvana. None of the famous sixteenth-century Spanish mystics allowed his private devotions to reduce in the slightest his duties in corporate worship. None felt that the church as an institution hindered in any way the fruition of his mystical experiences.

We have already suggested that a person anxiously seeking the mystic way might mistakenly convince himself or try to convince others that he has had mystical experiences. The ascetic, of course, faces the danger of coveting the rewards of virtue without acquiring a love of virtue itself.[7] A person does not need to be consciously seeking the label of ascetic or mystic in order to strive diligently to perform his religious duties. Surely few people have gone deeply into mystical experience. The desire, even the yearning for mystical experience will not of itself reach fruition. Many can go far enough in contemplation to convince themselves that a mystical experience is believable. Fray Luis de Granada was such a person. In all his writings which touch upon the mystic way, he never uses the first person. He apparently never felt that he himself had experienced a communion with God which could be reported as a personal experience for the education and inspiration of his readers.

Granada was primarily an ascetic. He had a tranquility of spirit that made the very stringent asceticism that he practiced seem like a surfeit of comfort. He recognized that virtue was not necessarily proportional to the severity of abstinence or penance. He had a gentle love for his fellow man that completely removed any image of the fanatic from the ascetic life. Therefore, he was an excellent guide for those who sought virtue in ascetic living. Granada was also a good guide for those who sought the mystic way. Perhaps his balanced, didactic attitude toward religion was better for the beginner in that style of life than were the writings of the great mystics themselves. And if a person recognized that he was not destined to have mystical experiences, he would find nothing in Granada's thoughts to nourish his disappointment, but on the contrary, might find many compensations in the other manifestations of God's love.

Fray Luis did not formally divide his teaching, as we have done here, into these two categories of Martha and Mary. He did imply from time to time that some people serve God better through action, others through contemplation, and that both types were to be encouraged to serve God in the way that they found most fulfilling.

III *Integration of the Two Previous Parts*

In the first part of this chapter we tried to give the religious background of Granada's life and writings by recalling the most significant events, the Protestant Reformation and the Erasmian reform. In the second part, we examined the scene from the point of view of certain aspects of individual religious experience in sixteenth-century Spain. It seems pertinent at this point to raise the question of the effect of the upper echelons of the church on Granada's mission of intellectual ministry to the humble Christian.

Fray Luis was always conscious of living in a structured society, and he liked it. His sharpest difference in personality from Erasmus was his reluctance to take an original or individual position. The church was one indivisible body. Those of religious profession were divided into various orders such as the Dominicans, Augustinians, Franciscans, and Carmelites, and even under the best of conditions, rivalries among the orders were inevitable; but one can get no hint of these rivalries from Granada's writings or from his acts. His thoughts were primarily directed to the cloister, but they needed no reinterpretation to have their influence on the hearth as well. There is no hint that he felt that celibacy was more pleasing to God than was holy matrimony.

I believe that the primary aim for Granada, perhaps subconsciously, was to keep the minds of his readers on what he considered important for them. Theological speculations or disputations of the church's leaders did not need to have any effect upon a simple man's duty to God, to his neighbor, and to himself. Granada felt that he could give these people practical advice for daily living, based upon his own education, but edited for their understanding, without discussing heresy and schism. He did not seek to warn his reader of the dangers to orthodoxy in his time. Instead, he warned the reader of the potency of sin while reassuring him of God's power and love.

Perhaps as a corollary to this point it should be added that Granada seemed to sense that there was a danger in overreacting to these protesting forces within and outside of Catholicism's realm. When Granada found out that two of his books were banned by the Inquisition, he remained calm. He did rush to the defense of these books, but he did not consider that his rights were being invaded nor did he think he was proclaiming erroneous doctrine. He simply rewrote them to make them conform to the Inquisition's standards, without abandoning any principle that lay behind his original ideology.

Granada himself recognized the delicacy of the problem of the impact that mystical writing might have in the context of the Northern Protestants, the Spanish *alumbrados,* and the negotiations at Trent. He felt that the spirit of private devotions and that of public religious practice could and should function in harmony. Mental prayer must lead to a deeper understanding of God, not to the disintegration of His church.

None of these problems seemed to restrict Granada's ability to formulate his message. His need to be cautious about what he wrote seemed only to make him think more thoroughly and more constructively about how to make his message effective. There is a possibility that the temporary setback at the hands of the Inquisition made him too cautious in the treatment of mystical matters. He insisted that vocal and mental prayer were essentially the same, despite the sharp contrast between them that most of his contemporaries were making. Often, apparently about to be swept up in mystical freedom, he would seem to deliberately plant his feet upon an ascetic *terra firma*. If this is a valid criticism, it comes from the point of view of the literary critic rather than the religious critic. Granada's message was for all people, but at times it seemed especially pertinent for the prosaic ones.

CHAPTER 2

Life of Fray Luis de Granada

I   The Making of a Preacher

A S Queen Isabella the Catholic reached her grave in 1504, Luis de Granada, another great Catholic was born.[1] His father, Francisco had taken his family name from the little Galician town of Sarriá. He had presumably moved to the southern city to seek a better fortune, but he died there when Luis was only five. The biographers do not tell us the name or the native city of Luis's mother. Perhaps she was also from Sarriá. When widowed, perhaps even before, she began to work as laundress to the Dominican monastery of Santa Cruz in Granada.

We are given only one note about Luis's childhood; oddly enough, it concerns a fight. Luis, in the shadow of the Alhambra was fighting with another boy when they were separated by the Count of Tendilla, warden of the city. The boy's righteous indignation greatly impressed the count, who made him page to his sons and allowed him to share their studies. One source, possibly an apocryphal one, tells us that Luis was defending the honor of his mother when his companion made insulting remarks about her poverty. One would like to believe that the story is literally true. It does offer a plausible explanation for the beginnings of Luis's education. Details of the training which qualified him for advanced scholarship are not known. Padre Cuervo states that Luis was very fond of listening to sermons and discussing them with his companions afterward.[2] Cuervo does not say how contagious his enthusiasm was except to note that his friends called him "the preacher."

Fray Luis entered the Dominican convent of Santa Cruz, where his mother had been laundress, in 1524 and made his profession June 15, 1525. José Joaquín de Mora reports that each Convent of that order was a kind of university.[3] In 1529, Luis received a fellowship for advanced study at the convent of San Gregorio, Valladolid. There, Cuervo tells us, he met the "very famous" Carranza and the "very wise" Melchor Cano.[4] San Gregorio must have been a remarkable place to study if its faculty contained such men as Carranza and Cano, the leading liberal and conservative theologians, respectively, of the country. Small wonder that under these conflicting influences Granada was to become the leading eclectic writer. It was here at Valladolid that he adopted the name of his native city as his own surname.

What he studied can best be determined from the names of the authors he cites in his books. His knowledge of the Holy Scripture and that of the church fathers seems almost inexhaustible. Among scores that he cites, one recognizes as of greater importance the names of Augustine, Gregory the Great, Bernard of Clairvaux, Thomas Aquinas, and Bonaventure. He used their works more to lend authority to his arguments than to display his erudition. He also studied the great pagan philosophers, among them Plato, Aristotle, Seneca, Cicero, and the Stoics. His use of their works shows that he must have had careful and enlightened teachers, and if conservative for our day, they were certainly liberal for his. For Granada and his contemporaries, philosophy was of course subordinated to faith and revelation. Fray Luis uses philosophical writings to supplement the revelations made to biblical and early Christian writers. Occasionally he observes, perhaps a little patronizingly, that these philosophers, limited as they were to human knowledge, were nevertheless able to reach a certain truth. Therefore, his reader, with the added benefit of Divine Illumination, should be able to grasp the truth quite readily. He nearly always selects from his sources those ideas with which he can agree. Only the Epicureans are regularly criticized adversely.

We can assume that his linguistic training was excellent. He showed his mastery of Latin by writing sermons in it, by translating works from Latin, and by writing a Latin treatise on rhetoric. In this treatise (and to some extent elsewhere) he showed his interest in the Greek language. Perhaps he knew Greek well enough to read Plato and Aristotle in the original. We know for certain only that he cites a large number of Greek terms for rhetorical and philosophical distinctions.

Granada's biological and astronomical knowledge was excellent for that day. Part of it, to be sure, was formed from reading such ancient authorities as Galen, Pliny, and Ptolemy, but much came from his own observations of nature. He was apparently not disturbed by discovering contradictions between knowledge gained from authorities and that obtained by personal observation. He accepted the authority of the ancient scientists as readily as that of the early theologians. Since his thoughts about nature were primarily intended to show the glory and providence of God, inaccuracy of detail and errors of scientific theory did not impair the lesson in morality taught his contemporaries. The use of personal knowledge of nature in his works was to increase steadily throughout Granada's life, culminating in the first part of the *Introducción del símbolo de la fe (Introduction to the Symbol of Faith)*.

Life in the monastery was no hardship for Fray Luis, since it obviously followed his own natural inclination. One story of his stay at Valladolid told by all early biographers will help reveal one of his rare qualities. In this incident two men, seeking night and solitude for immoral purposes, chose by chance a spot near where Fray Luis was whipping his own flesh to mortify and purge his soul. The men were struck by the contrast between their intentions and the punishment Fray Luis was giving himself and assumed that God's will had brought them there for a warning. They came to him the next day and made their confession, seeking his intercession with God for their forgiveness. We assume that Granada was glad to help these men, but his own reaction included seeking greater privacy for his self-inflicted penances.

Some confusion exists as to dates during Granada's middle years. Padre Cuervo has Granada leaving San Gregorio around 1534.[5] He returned to his convent, Santa Cruz, where he soon acquired fame as teacher and preacher. Eventually he acquired the title of master of theology, conferred by Fray Vicente Justiniano, leader of the Dominican order and later to become a cardinal. Granada, however, seems to have preferred the job of preacher, perhaps thereby feeling closer to the church's real mission. De Mora comments on the popularity of Fray Luis's preaching as well as its effectiveness, noting its beautiful simplicity in contrast to gongoristic preaching of a century later.[6] Granada's earliest biographer, Jerónimo Joannini, quoted by de Mora, says of his preaching:

His preaching was that of an evangelical man, seeking only to win souls and to plant the love of Heaven in the human breast. His voice was clear, soft, and sweet; he did not have to strive to acquire these qualities, since his words were naturally harmonious and penetrated the understanding of all who heard them. He showed that he was learned, capable of teaching and knowing how to express what he wished as appropriately and clearly as needed, adjusting to the understanding of his listeners. His concepts were all taken from the Holy Scripture, the best-known of the Holy Fathers, and Latin and Greek philosophers, and he wove of them the garland of his speech as if the concepts were all flowers. His style was pure, clean, simple but lofty, plain but meaningful, grave but graceful, florid but Christian, and attaining that fruitfulness which people everywhere said was great.[7]

It is interesting that his first triumphs as a preacher came back at Santa Cruz in Granada, since that city had retained much Moslem influence and some could still remember the war, some forty-five years before. Little that is definite has been recorded about Granada's first years of evangelical activity. One may assume that his work pleased common people and church authorities alike. Soon an assignment of great responsibility and difficulty was given him.

There was an old monastery near Córdoba founded in the reign of Juan II (1405–1454). This monastery, Scala Coeli, was a mountain retreat, and the Dominicans maintained an active group there for some time. But with passing time, religious fervor had cooled, and the place was virtually abandoned when Granada was called to be its prior and to revitalize it. The reestablishment order came in 1534, but it is not certain how soon this was carried out. Here was an unusual task for a man so young. The maintenance of a well-established monastery requires leadership and experience; the renewal of a failing organization must have been far more challenging. Yet, we learn that Granada soon found time to visit Córdoba and other nearby places, preaching the simple enthusiastic message which endeared him to all.

Scala Coeli, primitive and lonely in the Córdoban hills, seemed an ideal spot for a monastery. Perhaps here Fray Luis first began seriously to contemplate nature and to find in its contemplation an act of worship of the Creator. It was while there that he met Juan de Avila. This Andalusian ascetic, later beatified by the Church, was said to have had a profound influence upon Fray Luis. Avila was noted for his ability to reach the hearts of those outside the cloister. His rough, John-the-Baptist-like character complemented that of the gentler Granada, who was to become his biographer.

Granada spent some eight years at Scala Coeli. Presumably he left it in a condition of stability and active mission. A special friend of the Dominicans, the Duke of Medina Sidonia, invited Fray Luis to serve as chaplain at the ducal palace in Sanlúcar. Apparently the Duke expected to find urbanity in Granada's eloquence and a comforting sense of his presence. It may reasonably be assumed that he was not really seeking a man of Granada's austerity and deep commitment to Christianity. There was no quarrel reported between the two, but when the opportunity came to start a new monastery in Badajoz, on the Portuguese border, Fray Luis was eager to accept a new assignment, while the duke seemed equally pleased to further this new enterprise.

II *The Making of a Diplomat*

By the time Fray Luis de Granada reached Badajoz, at about the age of forty-five, he had achieved considerable fame as an accomplished pulpit orator, a fine administrator, and a holy man, even though as we now know, his major services to his God and his fellowman lay ahead. From Badajoz it was natural that his reputation should spread to Portugal, and after about six years in the border city, he was called to Portugal during a most intriguing era of Lusitanian history.

Fray Luis arrived shortly before the death of Portugal's King John III. The King's only son had died previously while his grandson and heir, Sebastian, was an infant. The affairs of the state were turned over to Catalina, John's widow, as queen regent. This remarkable woman was the sister of Charles V of Spain and granddaughter of Queen Isabella. Catalina's brother-in-law, Henry, was a cardinal and thus in a strategic spot for affairs of church and state. Another politically complicating factor was that Spain's Philip II was directly related to the Portuguese royal family through his mother.

On his first meeting with Fray Luis, the Portuguese Cardinal-Prince Henry asked Granada to be his confessor. Fray Luis respectfully declined the honor on the grounds that, as a newcomer to Portugal, he lacked proper orientation for the position. Presumably the cardinal, a circumspect man, realized that here was an unusually well-qualified man for future assignments, a man of rare ability, without a trace of vanity, and with little or no ambition for ecclesiastical honors. Granada was destined to spend the rest of his life in Portugal, with much of it devoted to Portuguese national affairs, especially those involving Castile.

Granada's orientation was fairly rapid. He accepted, with modesty and perhaps reluctance, the post of provincial of his order for the term 1556–1560. It must have been unusual to bestow this responsibility on one not Portuguese born, though it was still to be a number of years before Spanish-Portuguese relations reached their nadir. The period of Granada's tenure was one of considerable growth for the Dominican order in Portugal. Granada soon became confessor to Queen Catalina. She was a genuinely pious woman who wished to set a high moral tone for her country. She was anxious to have Fray Luis accept the post as bishop of Braga. Before his extreme reluctance to undertake this responsibility, she yielded to his wishes with his promise to help her persuade a pious and worthy man to accept. The man chosen was Granada's friend, Bartolomé de los Mártires. Fray Luis later wrote a biography of Fray Bartolomé. After Granada's term as provincial had ended, he chose as his residence the Convent of Santo Domingo in Lisbon.

Fray Luis changed residences from time to time, apparently basing his decision on whether administrative work or writing was his chief preoccupation. For a time he was at Setúbal where a monastery was being started amid delays and difficulties, but in 1569 he was in the monastery of the Sierra de Almeirin, to be available to the cardinal and to have leisure for writing.[8]

Meanwhile, Sebastian, the boy king, was growing up. As he reached adolescence, he began to feel more and more that his grandmother and his great uncle were filling the post he should be filling, and he especially resented the influence of the Spanish monk, Granada. When finally able to assume the throne at age eighteen, it was natural that Sebastian wished to undertake something melodramatic—an expedition to drive the infidel out of Africa. He received no help or encouragement from other European monarchs. His uncle, Philip II of Spain, was especially cool to the idea. The queen and Prince Henry tried to dissuade him, but he was headstrong and resolute. Sebastian led the Portuguese army to Africa and in August, 1578, suffered defeat and presumed death at Alcázar-Quivir. There is an interesting and durable legend that Sebastian escaped and returned to Portugal in disguise, but it is irrelevant to our story.

Six months before the African adventure came to its tragic end, Queen Catalina died. Granada preached the funeral oration, with Portuguese affairs in a state of near chaos. The old cardinal became

Portugal's king, but there was no heir apparent. Besides Don Antonio de Sousa, whose claims were marred by illegitimate birth, there were two other claimants to the throne: Philip II of Spain, whose maternal grandfather had been Portugal's King Manuel, and the Duchess of Braganza. The duchess had the disadvantage of being female. Her only advantage was that she was truly Portuguese. In addition to his masculine advantage, Philip II had an army. Since Philip's uncle was old and a celibate, the Spanish monarch was willing to bide his time, but it was clear to all that he expected to become king of Portugal.

The Portuguese patriots were left with one forlorn hope. If the cardinal would consent to marry and could get a dispensation to do so, he might become a father despite his almost seventy years. Philip II was not blind to that possibility, remote as it was. He sent a secret ambassador, Fray Hernando de Castillo, with the purpose of dissuading his uncle from marriage. To conceal the true purpose of his mission, the announcement was made that Castillo was to visit Fray Luis, the two being natives of the city of Granada.

Granada's biographer, Father Cuervo, devotes a great deal of space to the negotiations during Castillo's visit.[9] The situation was, of course, pathetic. Obviously the cardinal did not want to marry. Castillo wished to discover how strong the movement was to get the king to marry. He reported to Philip that King Henry had told him everyone was urging him as a patriotic duty to marry, and that consequently he planned to do so, despite his personal feelings. On the other hand, Castillo obtained from Fray Luis the view that only a few were pressing on this matter, and that most thought the idea to be nonsense. One is tempted to think that King Henry deliberately exaggerated the possibility of marriage in his interview with Castillo in order to make Philip nervous, but Granada tells us that the monarch was so disturbed by the thought of marriage that he became seriously ill.[10] His first sign of illness was a hemorrhage of the mouth. When the doctors reported to King Henry that he should not marry, he was relieved and consoled, considering his illness a sign from God. The recovery of his spirit came too late; he went to his grave shortly afterward. Biographers report no formal plea to the Holy See for dispensation, nor is any woman mentioned who might have been selected to become his wife.

Before his death King Henry appointed a regency commission to determine his successor. This group must have realized that if they

chose Philip II, they would run counter to patriotic pride. If they
defied the Spanish king, Portugal would be crushed with overwhelming force. They were therefore slow to act, but Philip was
not. He quickly dispatched the Duke of Alva with an army to Lisbon. Orders within Portugal generally were not to oppose the
Spaniards and resistance was nominal. The commission did have to
flee Lisbon for safety from the local patriots.

Much of the opposition to Philip, feeble as it was, came from the
Dominicans, and Philip was in no mood to tolerate any vestige of
Portuguese nationalism. In the center of the Dominican Order's
politics in late 1580 was a vacancy as vicar general. The man chosen
was Fray Antonio de la Cerda, who proved an unpopular choice; he
satisfied neither patriots nor those who favored Philip. Granada's
disappointment with the choice became known. At this point a mysterious brief called a *motu proprio* arrived, allegedly sent by the
pope, replacing Antonio de la Cerda with Fray Luis de Granada.[11]
It was evidently a forgery, perpetrated by someone or some group
opposed to Philip. The mystery was never solved. For a time the
royal wrath was directed against Fray Luis, who was ordered to
ignore the brief and summoned before the king, even though it
meant an absurdly difficult trip for him. The strong intercession of
the Duke of Alva and the conciliatory tone of Granada's replies
helped reduce Philip's rage. Eventually, the king reached Lisbon
and hearing Granada preach, lost all vestiges of animosity, and even
visited him in his cell. Even if Philip had not been convinced of the
loyalty of Fray Luis's heart, the infirmity of his body should have
convinced him that he could not be an effective enemy of the
Spanish crown.

III   *Granada as a Writer*

Fray Luis de Granada's importance as a writer far surpasses the
other accomplishments noted above. He published his first work in
Seville in 1538, a translation into Spanish of the *Contemptus
mundi.*[12] Instead of "contempt for the world" this work is generally
known today by a subtitle *La imitación de Cristo (The Imitation of
Christ)*. It is attributed to the Dutch monk Thomas à Kempis and
has had a powerful hold upon the conscience of the faithful ever
since the fifteenth century. Each of its four parts is composed of a
group of loosely connected aphorisms emphasizing the essential
baseness of man and the redeeming promises of Christ. Reading and

meditating upon this work is the mental equivalent of the corporal punishment ascetics were wont to give themselves. One reason for its power was the author's complete humility. It is obvious that he places himself on the same level with all other sinners. The book is the quintessence of medieval asceticism, appearing just before the dawn of the Renaissance.

Granada's translation was not the first Spanish version, but apparently the first good one.[13] In slightly revised form it is still printed today (along with newer versions).[14] This book must have made a profound impression upon him, but it is quite different in style and tone from Granada's own compositions. The style of Kempis is measured, polished, succinct; that of Granada is naturally exuberant, spontaneous, free-flowing. It was to be sixteen years before he would publish an original work, so one must conclude that the publication of *The Imitation of Christ* did not make him think that writing was to be his own special calling.[15]

It is unusual that so prolific a writer should have launched what was to become his definitive career at the late age of fifty. His first original work, *Libro de la oración y meditación (Book of Prayer and Meditation)*, appeared in its first version in 1554, followed by the *Guía de pecadores (Sinner's Guide)* in 1556. In this year he became provincial of the Dominicans in Portugal, and in 1559 suffered the setback of having his two books placed on the *Index* of the Inquisition.

Even those who accept wholeheartedly the principles upon which the Inquisition worked are likely to agree that the *Index* of 1559 was an example of excessive zeal. In the volume which is an anthology of Granada's works in the *Biblioteca de autores cristianos (Collection of Christian Authors)*, a sort of apology for the Inquisitor Fernando Valdés appears.[16] In it Fray Díez de Triana points out the dangers of Protestantism from without and, more poignantly, the *alumbrados* within. It was probably under the influence of these dangers that Valdés allowed his zeal to become excessive. Later, approval for the *Book of Prayer* for the reading public was obtained at the Council of Trent and ratified by Pope Pius IV. Granada always regarded the Inquisition as a proper instrument of the church. Father Cuervo offers a detailed account of Granada's relations with the Inquisition.[17]

Fray Luis revised slightly the first version of the *Book of Prayer and Meditation (Libro de la oración y meditación)*. He clarified a few passages to remove any language suggesting the "sterile quietism" of which it had been accused.[18] He completely rewrote the *Sinner's Guide*, removing the translations of the Scriptures (translating the Scriptures into the vernacular was considered dangerous by the inquisitors), and greatly enlarging the book in scope and content. Father Cuervo refers to the first edition as the compendium of the *Sinner's Guide*. This, while not quite accurate, serves to emphasize the larger size and scope of the revised edition. The expanded work as we know it today appeared in 1567. Never again was Fray Luis bothered by restrictions upon the publication of his books. There was a brief period in 1576 when a friend of his, Fray Alonso de la Fuente, having discovered a colony of *alumbrados* in Llerena, became a fanatic himself in denouncing the group and listed Granada's *Book of Prayer and Meditation* as a contributing element in heresy.[19] This denunciation apparently had little effect upon the world of the religious.

How could Granada have written so many books? A typical day in his life, recounted by most of his biographers, is as follows:

He would arise at four o'clock and spend two hours in prayer, preparing for mass. After mass, he and a stenographer companion would read for an hour. Then Fray Luis would dictate. At about eleven, he would relieve his companion and do his own writing. After dinner he engaged in community work or did further reading. He then visited the sick and followed that with a short recreation period, in conversation with his brothers. Then came a very short rest. Next the prayer of *nones* and further work until dark. A light supper and prolonged prayer completed the day at about eleven.[20]

Two notes are given us regarding his eating habits. One is that he was accustomed to giving a large portion of his food to the poor. The other is that he would have someone read to him while he was eating. In spite of his frugality, he feared abandoning his thoughts, even for a few moments, to the idle pleasure of consuming food.

The Inquisitor Valdés referred to Granada's works as "contemplation for carpenters' wives."[21] It was an unfortunate choice of words, especially since the Virgin Mary belonged to that category, but it helps us to place in focus the meaning of the life and works of Fray Luis de Granada. Sixteenth-century Europeans could be divided into two classes: those who could read Latin and those who could not. Latin readers tended to consider themselves guardians of all important knowledge and wisdom. It was they who made the interpretations of the meaning of everything vital for the church. Latin writings contained subtleties which they felt would baffle and confuse ordinary people. But the miracle of the printing press was gradually democratizing education. Books were becoming easier to obtain, and it was almost inevitable that many should be published in the vernacular.

Never for a moment did Fray Luis forget his humble origin, and despite the fact that he learned to master Latin and all the theological subtleties that it protected, he wished with a fervent heart to dedicate his life to the instruction and the spiritual well-being of those people not fortunate enough to acquire the education that he had received. At first he was content to preach and minister to them, but later he saw that the power of the printed word could multiply his effectiveness. He was modest, cautious, and diplomatic, but he remained steadfast in this principle. The son of a laundress would interpret the Scriptures for nuns, monks, and wives of carpenters.

The first need that Granada saw and tried to fulfill was a guide for prayer and meditation. He thus began with his *Book of Prayer and Meditation*. Later, he wrote other works on prayer leading to a mystical interpretation of life. First among these was the *Memorial de la vida cristiana* (*Memorial of Christian Life*, 1566); while for those more advanced in contemplative worship he wrote the *Adiciones al memorial de la vida cristiana* (*Additions to the Memorial of Christian Life*, 1574). Meanwhile, he provided a general guide to virtuous living in the *Guía de pecadores (Sinner's Guide)*. [22]

Finally, in 1582, he published the first four volumes of the *Introducción del símbolo de la fe (Introduction to the Symbol of Faith)*. The fifth volume, composed in 1585 when Granada was over eighty, is a compendium of the first four. This work is not exactly an ascetic work as was the *Sinner's Guide*, nor is it a mystical one. It is, rather, a theological treatise, but with an approach so different from the usual theological work that it seems in a class by itself. It is a treatise upon sources of faith: nature, which shows the providence of God; the history of Christianity with its stories of martyrs, illustrating its superiority over the world's other religions; the relationship between original sin and the Cross; the history of the Old Testament as God's preparation for Christianity, and as a prophesy of the coming of the Savior. While it has not achieved the popularity of the *Sin-*

ner's Guide, from the standpoint of literary art and originality many may consider it their favorite.

Granada's writings are in three languages. He has several volumes of sermons and a book on rhetoric written in Latin. He also wrote one work in Portuguese: *Compendio de doctrina christiána (Compendium of Christian Doctrine).* This was written expressly because of the shortage of preachers in the mountains of the Braga diocese, and undoubtedly for that reason it is more basic and elementary in form and content than are his other works, though style and pedagogical techniques are quite similar. The book begins with a catechism including the Creed, the Lord's Prayer, the Ave María, the Salve, the Ten Commandments, and a listing of the various virtues and vices. Next, he gives a long explanation of the meaning of the Creed after dividing it into twelve parts to facilitate his analysis. As a pedagogical device, he names each part after one of the apostles. These twelve parts are subdivided into three segments: an explanation of their meaning and significance, a practical application of this faith, and the harm coming from disbelief or malpractice. As usual, he amazes by the details provided to substantiate his points. The same manner used for instruction on the Creed is repeated for his lesson on the Ten Commandments and the seven deadly sins. The third part of the work discusses prayer, ending with a description and explanation of the Sacraments.

There is no difference in spirit between the Portuguese *Compendio* and Granada's Castilian writings. Evidently it is called a compendium either because it summarizes much previously written in Castilian, or to emphasize its small, convenient size. It is not a compendium of a particular work. It deals primarily with explanation of church dogma, but can still be used as source material for meditation. It shows that for Fray Luis, even on the most elementary level, all approaches to the meaning and practice of Christian life are useful and in harmony. Although he was asked to translate this work into Castilian, he never found time to do so, and it was translated shortly after his death by Fray Enrique de Almeyda.

In addition to the writings mentioned, Fray Luis wrote two biographies, *Juan de Avila* and *Bartolomé de los Mártires,* and did a translation of the *Scala paradisi (Spiritual Ladder)* by St. John Climacus, as well as a translation of a letter of Eucherius, Bishop of Lyon, appended to the *Sinner's Guide,* and various compendia or summaries of works mentioned above. Of these, the biography of

Bartolomé de los Mártires is the one which has commanded most attention.

For those interested in his Latin works, it is not necessary to know Latin. The *Biblioteca de autores españoles (Collection of Spanish Authors)* has thirteen sermons and Granada's book on rhetoric available in Spanish translation.[23]

IV *The Venerable Father Granada*

By the time he was eighty, Granada's respected place in the religious and political history of Spain and Portugal was assured. He was beloved of king and beggar, of saint and sinner. Such a person can never rest, for he becomes the victim of his own fame. Fray Luis would have become uncomfortable at the thought that he would be considered more holy than an ordinary man. He would no more have wanted posthumous honors that the bishopric he declined. He knew what happens to those who succumb to the sin of pride. The church has declared him venerable; surely he is worthy of that title.

An incident which occurred late in his life shows the great strength of his character, even at that advanced age. A Lisbon woman, María de la Visitación, prioress of a convent, was achieving considerable fame as a mystic. She claimed to have had frequent visitation from Christ, including the imprint of His wounds in her feet, hands, and side.[24] Those who doubted the validity of her claims also received considerable publicity. Fray Luis, perhaps through chivalry, perhaps through a natural desire to believe that a person is truthful in matters of such utter seriousness, defended her, rebuking those who expressed disbelief in her statements. A thorough investigation showed, however, not only that her visitations were false, but that their fabrication was childish, the product of a severe inferiority complex. She was persuaded to confess.

If pride was not one of Granada's sins, chagrin could not mortify him either. He was inspired to preach what is probably his best-known sermon, "against the scandals of those who fall from public trust." Granada reminded his listeners that faith in a mortal is different from faith in God. Faith in God should always be above faith in any creature. Every human being is, after all, no more than human, and the example of human failure should not discourage one who seeks the path to virtue.

Though his last years were plagued by declining health, he continued to preach. Part of his success as a preacher was due to the moving quality of his voice, a quality able to transcend even the loss of teeth. His last years were made pleasant by letters and visits from his many friends and admirers. Among these letters, two deserve special mention: one is from St. Theresa de Jesus, Spain's great mystic, and the other is from Pope Gregory XIII.

There is a description by the eighteenth-century biographer Luis Muñoz, who apparently writes of Fray Luis at the height of his physical powers, which is so widely quoted that it seems almost like an official word portrait:

He was majestic, above average in height, large-boned, heavily built. His face had an angelic peacefulness, his complexion soft, delicate, of good color; his eyes were small but merry and modest, placed continually on the ground; his forehead, spacious and serene, its lines, together with the straightness of his nose, formed a star; his teeth were white and regular, his nose aquiline, fairly large, a feature highly esteemed by the Persians (it had among them a sign of regal bearing), a small mouth, his hair was once blondish, later white, his head thick, somewhat bald. He was very sweet in his conversation and a friend of all.[25]

The year 1588 was the one in which Spaniards were wondering about the meaning of the defeat of the "invincible armada," but nothing in Granada's biography indicates that he was troubled over such worldly concerns. His last conversation was with the novices of his monastery. At this point he knew that his death was approaching, and he was prepared for it. He died three hours before the New Year of 1589 and was buried on the afternoon of New Year's Day.

An account of his burial will help us to picture the feeling that the common people had for him:

The burial was held at four o'clock in the afternoon of the New Year, and it moved all the city and its environs. There were so many people that they scarcely let us bury him, and such was the devotion of the people that they struggled to get to see him and kiss his clothes and touch rosaries to his face; and when we were reaching the tomb they kept cutting his cloak and garments for relics so that they almost cast him nude into the tomb, and if the monks had not defended him, not a thread of clothing would remain; even the single tooth that he had in life was taken from him in death.[26]

The last years of Granada's life were among the greatest for Christianity since the first century of the Christian era. In Spain this period produced St. John of the Cross, the most sublime of all mystic poets, St. Theresa de Jesus, the most human, best-known, and most beloved of all saintly women after the Holy Virgin, Fray Luis de León, Spain's favorite religious poet, and many lesser ones. Literary history accords a more prominent place to some of these than to Fray Luis de Granada, but it is doubtful that any reflected better the spirit of the age in its religious attitude. To know Granada is to know the kindness, humility, and purity of heart which that age was capable of showing. Since he was the oldest of those of highest rank, he contributed in large measure, both by his life and by his writings, to the spirit of the age and to the inspiration of its leaders. St. Theresa, especially, admired his works and wrote him of her esteem, stating that she asked her Creator to grant him a long life for the writing of works of devotion. As seen above, her prayer was granted.

CHAPTER 3

Sinner's Guide

THE *Sinner's Guide* is Granada's masterpiece, although students of mysticism may prefer the books that we will examine in Chapter 4. The literary critic may admire more the *Introduction to the Symbol of Faith*. The *Sinner's Guide*, however, is the work most often printed and seems to be considered as Granada's most representative.[1] It emphasizes, more than his other writings do, the diversity of ways of serving God and the unity, within this diversity, of the Christian life. Its appeal is directed to man's sense of justice and reasonableness. While it has an emotional tone as do all of Granada's works, that tone is somewhat muted here.

The edition which we will discuss is the revised edition that appeared in 1567 and which is universally recognized as the definitive one.[2] There are two major changes between the first edition (1556) and that of 1567. The first edition had a translation of the Sermon on the Mount as illustrative material. The revised edition omits this material entirely. In its place Granada enlarges the scope of the work, adding new didactic material. A comparison of the two editions has been undertaken recently by Marcel Bataillon and Dámaso Alonso.[3] Their work demonstrates that the influence which Erasmus exerted upon Granada was growing during this period, despite increased activity by the Inquisition.

Granada probably thought of *Sinner's Guide* somewhat as we think of a textbook. It can be divided into units of appropriate size for studying. It lends itself to summarizing or to memorizing of excerpts representing the whole, and can be reviewed easily without losing the transition. We will emphasize this pedagogical organization, even at the risk of monotony in the seemingly endless, rhythmic beat of his classifications.

40

I *Prologue and Organization*

At the beginning of the book there is a justifying prologue *(pró- logo galeato)*. In it Granada stresses the importance of the written word as a bulwark against the powers of sin. By descriptions and analogies, he virtually calls the written word a weapon to use in defense of the faith. This weapon is of no value unless the Christian knows how to use it. Granada claims that Jews and Moslems know the doctrines of their faiths better than Christians do their own. If the Christian does not know God's will as expressed in Christian doctrine, how can he serve God properly? Fray Luis stresses the importance of doctrinal knowledge by comparing it to a clock with interlocking wheels. The wheel of knowledge moves all of the other wheels that move the body. Knowledge is like the eyes of the body. Samson, says Granada, was blinded by the Philistines to render him helpless. A Christian without knowledge of the doctrines of his faith is equally blind. He points out that Jesus used his knowledge of (Jewish) doctrine to fight temptation in the wilderness (Matthew 4:4).

Granada shows his awareness of the danger of exposing the un- sophisticated to biblical passages which are obscure and therefore may be misunderstood, thereby accepting criticism of the first edi- tion of his *Sinner's Guide*. He points out that those who do not read Latin and therefore do not have direct access to the Bible, do need to receive special instruction on such subjects as confession and prayer. He expresses the hope that those who read his book will acquire four virtues: love of God, hatred of sin, hope in divine mercy, and fear of divine justice.

At the end of the prologue is found a technique often employed by Granada, a sort of rebuttal against objections which have been raised or which he imagines may be raised against the purposes of this book. One of these is the idea that the book may not be in harmony with sermons the reader may hear from time to time. Fray Luis, however, fears that these sermons may not fully meet the spiritual needs of the sinners to whom this book is directed. He believes that the effect of reading his book will be that a person will listen more closely to sermons, not that he will ignore them or be confused by comparing the book with sermons. Granada considers the possibility that errors of misinterpretation may be made, but

believes this a calculated risk; in general, the reader should be
enlightened far more than he is confused or led astray. The prologue
can be considered not only as a justification for writing this *Sinner's
Guide*, but as a general apology for writing devotional books in the
vernacular.

The *Sinner's Guide* is divided into two Books. Book I in turn is
divided into three parts and Book II into two parts. Each Book is
also divided into chapters, numbered consecutively without regard
to the division into parts (thirty and twenty-three chapters respectively). Certain chapters are then subdivided into numbered sections, some with, some without titles. Book I has a brief summary
(*argumento*) at the beginning. Each of the ten chapters of the first
part of Book I represents a title (*título*) or reason, calling man to a
life of virtue. The first two chapters in the second part bring the
number of titles to an even dozen and are matched by twelve more
chapters, each describing the rewards of practicing these virtues.
The third part is Granada's answer to those men who find excuses
for not following the path of virtue, and finally, Chapter XXX serves
as the conclusion to Book I. Book II, which is much shorter, begins
with thirteen chapters (Part I) which discuss vices and how to guard
against them, and ends with ten chapters (Part II) offering specific
suggestions for the practice of each of the virtues.

This outline of the *Sinner's Guide*, easily formed from the chapter
titles, shows an approximate balance between the emphasis upon
the exhortation to virtue and guidance in its attainment, and negative warnings against sin with positive encouragement in the practice of virtue. The discussion of sin is postponed until after the
reader has been encouraged to think positively about virtue. The
practice of virtue, however, is placed at the end so that the entire
work concludes on an optimistic note. The *Sinner's Guide* thus has
an appealing symmetry, adding beauty to utility, since the main
purpose surely was for the sinner to find ease in learning, reviewing,
and retaining its contents.

In general Book I outlines what God does for every person. The
creation, redemption, justification, and general sustaining help are
offered by God to all of his creatures who formally accept Him. The
mercies of God disclosed here are not measured according to man's
worthiness but according to his need. All ultimately look to the
rewards or punishments of the everlasting life.

Book II has a different emphasis. It deals with the special help

God gives those who try to live virtuously. With the exception of one chapter, it is confined to man's spiritual well-being, largely in its day by day application. Granada wishes to show his reader that the path of virtue is good for its own sake, not just for the rewards at the end, even though these rewards are important. For Granada, a life of virtue is self-fulfillment, not self-denial. A person is happier on the road to virtue than he is on the road to pleasure, because the joys of virtue grow, while those of the pleasure seekers prove deceptive or at best ephemeral.

II *The First Chapter: God Is Infinity*

It is my intent to summarize the first chapter more thoroughly so that it may serve as an example of the structure and spirit of the rest. Granada's works are too numerous and too vast to permit an examination in as much detail as one might like. It is not merely that this chapter is the first; it contains some of the most impressive thoughts of Fray Luis, exemplifying his finest ways of expressing them.

Fray Luis begins by telling his reader that in his conduct man possesses a twofold motivation: his sense of duty, and his hope of reward. He believes that duty should be the stronger of the two. He tries to make duty pleasant by telling the reader that he is called to a life of virtue in the service of God because of who God is. Granada tries to give us a concept of God by comparing our limitations with God's infinite qualities. Creatures can have distinguishable parts: they can grow, change, and increase their possessions. By contrast, all of God's characteristics merge in infinity. Therefore his mercy and his justice are the same. His goodness, beauty, and wisdom are all one. Punishment and forgiveness are the same to God. How then should one think of God? How can we picture Him? Granada suggests that we follow St. Augustine in thinking of God as a light superior to all earthly lights; a light that the eyes do not see; or as a voice superior to all earthly sounds, a voice that the ears do not hear. In this way God is not considered as having any special form. With Dionysius, Fray Luis says that as we think of God we should be silent instead of using our voices to praise Him, for just as light is indivisible, so is silence. Thus silence is a symbol of infinity. This should be considered within the context of one who is alone contemplating God and striving for a vivid image of His nature, not as a method of public worship.

St. Thomas Aquinas is Granada's guide for further attempts to

compare the limitations of man in quality and in size to the Al-
mighty. Granada asks us to consider the four elements in their order
of excellence with earth, the lowest element, followed by water, air,
and fire respectively. Next come the circles of heaven, ten in
number, each one larger than its predecessor, and finally the empy-
rean beyond all. To contemplate the size of man within the universe, Granada asks us to recall that astrologers say that there are
stars eighty times the size of the sun. The contemplation of this
contrast between God and man should, therefore, serve by itself
alone to move a man to a life of virtue. A man should consider, as
David did, that all of his sins against individuals, such as the virtual
murder of Uriah when David coveted his wife, Bathsheba, should
be considered as sins against God alone. If one accepts this reasoning, the obligation to seek the life of virtue should be irresistible.

At this early point in *Sinner's Guide*, one can already see much of
the working of Granada's mind. He is attuned to speculative and
imaginative reasoning, but his thoughts are carefully controlled by
his educational background and his respect for authority. He de-
duces ideas about infinity from statements about finite things, establishing hierarchies and making comparisons from them. He quotes
from authorities, both Christian and classical, while making clear his
belief that the classical authority had only human reasoning to guide
him while the Christian had divine Revelation. One can already
begin to see the eclectic in him as he chooses his references freely:
from the Bible, from the Church Fathers, quoting as liberally from
St. Augustine as from St. Thomas Aquinas, from Plato and Aristotle,
with no sign that he was concerned about the philosophical differences between them. In the use of patristic writings, there is no sign
that he favored the Dominican Order over its rivals. There is an
eclectic spirit also in the question of whether to warn or reassure, to
use intellect or passion, to appeal to reason or to cite authority.

III   *Chapters II–VI: God's Power to Help Us in Life*

Chapters II–VI continue the exposition of reasons why man
should be moved to a life of virtue because of what God is or has
done for us. They represent an effort to explain theological concepts
in a language that the unsophisticated can understand, and to avoid
the theological niceties that Granada must have deemed unnecessary to his purpose. These chapters concern, respectively, God as

Creator, providence, guarantor of our redemption, justification, and predestination.

In Chapter II Granada suggests that we are moved to seek virtue since God is our Creator. He created our bodies with their senses and our souls with their powers. Furthermore, Granada suggests that creation was not instantaneous, but is continuous. We need to return to God and remain close to Him, so that His task of finishing our creation can be successfully accomplished and so that our needs may be sustained: "If an image lacked eyes, would it seek kings or the sculptor who made it?" In gratitude to his Creator he would seek to live as God would have him live. This thought that the creation of man is a continuing process, so different from the Protestant concept of "the faith once and for all times delivered to the saints," shows the harmony of the Church's position theologically with Granada's technique pedagogically. If growth is important in many areas of life, it is helpful to think of creation as a process of growth. It seems to me to come surprisingly close to modern ideas of Christian existentialism. It was a happy turn of Granada's line of thought, and illustrates the flexibility of his mind and the breadth of his training.

The third chapter deals with the providence of God and man's duty to be grateful for it. The providential care of God is shown in all the natural wealth of the world, given for man's sustenance and pleasure. As examples of gratitude, Fray Luis cites stories of lions, including the one aided by Androcles; and for loyalty, examples of dogs who did not abandon their masters, even at the master's death. If animals, with only their instincts, show gratitude, should man not go further in showing his gratitude? The thought that man might be ungrateful creates in Granada a strong emotional feeling, contrasting with his usual calm, but he soon returns to his reasoned analysis. For example, citing Seneca, he speaks of degrees of ingratitude, the first of which is not to respond with good works, the second to forget the benefactor completely, the third to return evil for good. He warns the reader not to await the approach of death in order to reject these evils.

In Chapter IV Granada discusses his next reason for a call to virtue, which is in gratitude to God for our redemption. The discussion takes the reader into the life, death, and resurrection of Christ. Again, Fray Luis becomes emotional, and some of his remarks are addressed to God instead of to the reader. How can Granada express adequately Christ's thirty-three years of suffering for man's sake? While Granada feels his inadequacy of talent, he believes that keeping silent in the face of man's need to show his gratitude for his redemption would be far worse.

Chapter V explains the doctrine of justification and man's call to a life of virtue in gratitude for it. Granada speaks of the working of the Holy Spirit in men's lives and the sustaining force of the Holy Communion and other Sacraments. He does not, as some men did and do, make a doctrinal distinction between justification and sanctification but treats the terms largely as synonymous. For the church, the God that justifies man makes him just. Those who die redeemed but not yet justified, go to Purgatory to complete their justification. Granada does not reject the concept of Purgatory but shows little interest in discussing it and so confines his discussion of justification to the sustaining power of God's Church and of the Holy Spirit throughout life. If his reader will think about this blessing and try to show gratitude through seeking a life of virtue, he can of himself do no more.

Chapter VI deals with predestination as one of the blessings for which one should be grateful to God and thus inspired to a life of virtue. It is a simple but skillful presentation. Man was chosen *ab eterno* ("from the beginning of time") for salvation and each person is given "sufficient aid for his salvation." Granada warns that one should not, for this reason, take salvation for granted, but one may humbly assume that he is of the number who are to be saved. With that reassurance he presumably can serve God without an anxious thought about his own destiny. Granada's explanation of predestination does not deny free will; he does not try to explain or even acknowledge the problem of reconciling the theological antinomy between predestination and free will. He simply tells his reader that it is God's will for him to be saved and that he should be moved to seek virtue in gratitude to Him. The idea that predestination and free will could be mutually exclusive could disturb the reasoning of a theologian, but for Granada it seems to disappear before a kind of intuitive treatment, guided by faith.

IV *Chapters VII–X: God and Man's Death*

The last four chapters in the first part deal with the eschatological considerations: death, the last Judgment, the joys of Paradise, and the torments of Hell. In this context it is natural to assume that

death will have an ominous and gloomy aspect. Fray Luis tries hard
to keep the material of these four chapters from excessive overlapping. This is difficult since the thoughts of one category naturally
lead into the next.

The chapter on death stresses the pain of severance from relatives
and friends. It dwells also upon the uncertainty of the hour of death
and on the fact that it is likely to be preceded by sickness and
suffering. It gives a number of case histories of those who feared
death. For example, there is one cited by St. Gregory. The saintly
men each day ask themselves whether this day might be their last
and whether they are ready to face death. If they are comforted by
the thought that they have committed no evil deed, they then ask
themselves whether evil thoughts can have slipped in, since the
overcoming of evil thoughts is much more difficult for them than
overcoming the temptation to evil actions.

If we are to evaluate Granada's views on death largely on the basis
of the thoughts expressed in this chapter, we must bear in mind that
in the context of making men aware of the need to follow a life of
virtue he stresses the more fearful aspects of death. If he were
comforting a person at the hour of death, he would use a different
approach. These thoughts certainly contrast with those of some mystics, such as St. Theresa, who longed for death to be with Christ.
Granada regularly writes of principles, seldom of personal attitudes.
One gets the feeling that he is so sure of God's presence in man's
mortal existence that death, the transfer from mortality to immor-
tality, is not too important. To a person not living a righteous life it
is, of course, of great importance, but Granada seemed to have faced
his own death as one who realized he had lived long enough and
could say with the poet Jorge Manrique that "for man to wish to live
when God wants him to die is madness."

In Chapter VIII Fray Luis deals with the Day of Judgment. Actually there are two judgments: the individual judgment pronounced
at death and the final Judgment Day for the Universe. The reader's
attention is directed to the individual judgment. To emphasize the
awe of the moment, Granada seems to strip away all thoughts of
intercessors. The man who in the privacy of the confessional is afraid
to recount his sins will be alone before God with all his unconfessed
sins overwhelming him. The stress at this point is not upon the
tortures of Hell, the subject for Chapter X, but rather on the self-
torture of the one who reflects upon his sins and the awesome

experience of facing God. The reader may possibly feel that Granada missed the opportunity of emphasizing how much lighter the burden of the virtuous man would be. That, of course, is his implication, but he usually hammers out his persuasive reasons rather than leaving them to be inferred. He is a person of balance and eclectic thinking who nonetheless at many points becomes a debater, looking carefully at one side of a problem.

In his discussion of the rewards of Paradise, in Chapter IX, Fray Luis seems a little unsure of what to say. It is obvious to him that the joys of Heaven must vastly exceed the power of words to describe them. He contrasts earthly rewards, incomplete and temporal, with Paradise, complete and eternal. He compares the afterlife with the present life as proportional to the gain in quality of life outside of the womb with that within. The beauty of the earth is a pale suggestion of the beauty of Heaven. Probably, describing Heaven was no easy task for his mentors either.

This chapter emphasizes the presence of God in two ways: first, God is the planner of Heaven. We can trust Him to provide for man the best possible place of eternal rest. Second, the blessed will enjoy the beatific vision. Granada calls upon St. Augustine to describe the joy of the eternal vision of God which the blessed enjoy. Along with Dante and other Christian writers, Granada is superimposing the Christian Heaven upon the Ptolomaic astronomical heaven. While in Chapter I Granada spoke of the nine Heavens, there is nothing here to suggest that there are greater and lesser stations in Heaven. When he speaks of the blessed, therefore, he must be referring to all souls that are there.

Chapter X presents contemplation of the punishments of Hell, although Granada continues talking about God. It is clear that God is in control of man's punishment. The person who may be on the path to Hell is asked first to consider God's greatness, his mercy, his patience, the ingratitude of the wicked, and only after all this contrasting of divine goodness and human evil is the reader asked to think upon the executioner of God's judgment; that is, the Devil. As examples of torments and tormenters he quotes the ninth chapter of the Book of Revelation which deals with the torment of locusts. He refers to Isaiah, chapter thirty-three, for the symbol of punishment by eternal fire, and Isaiah 66:24 for the torment of the worm of remorse which eternally gnaws at its victim. Fray Luis emphasized the importance of eternity for the blessings of Paradise. The eternity of punishment seems even more poignant. If one could look forward to some relief, he says, even after a hundred thousand years, the ray of hope would be comforting. But Hell means eternity without change.

For moderns, perhaps the most interesting thing about Fray Luis's concept of Hell is the thought that even here God is in control. A soul in Hell is not thought of as one that the Devil has won from God in a battle. A lost soul is apparently one in which the individual, exercising his free will, has stubbornly refused divine aid. It is God who condemns man after exhausting His efforts to redeem him.

At this point the first part of Book I ends. It is a reasonable stopping point. The call to virtue has been presented both as an obligation of love and as a practical course of action for the believing Christian. Some concepts of Christian doctrine are explained in a way that is easy to understand and, more important, perhaps, hard for an impressionable reader to resist. Granada certainly expects his reader to continue by reading the second and third parts and thereafter of Book II, but if the reader is obliged to drop out at this point, there is a sense of an initial lesson completed.

V *Book I, Part II: God's Blessings to the Virtuous*

As Part II begins, the reader is confronted with some confusion as to numbers and organization. Part II begins with Chapter XI. Chapters XI and XII continue a numbered listing of the reasons for man's obligation to follow virtue, started in Part I. Chapter XII serves a dual purpose in his numbering system because for Granada the twelfth reason man is obligated to follow virtue is also the first of twelve privileges of virtue. Chapters XIII–XXIII then contain the other eleven privileges of virtue. One possible reason for this peculiar numbering system is that Fray Luis has only twenty-three chapters in Parts I and II, but wants the obligations and privileges to number twelve each. The obligations concern mainly man's relationship to eternal life and the privileges, to matters of his earthly existence, but the twelfth obligation is specifically gratitude for temporal blessings. Perhaps that is why it is placed in Part II instead of Part I.

In Chapter XI Granada tries to convince the reader that the road to virtue is not unpleasant. If virtue seems harsh and its rewards seem to lie in the distant future, perhaps the reader has not learned to appreciate the temporal blessings which flow from it. Virtue thus may resemble the images called "Sileni," rough and ugly on the outside, but whose inner value must be apparent to the one who seeks it.[4] In this chapter it must be confessed that Granada seems to ramble rather badly. He definitely wishes to convey the idea that the quest for virtue is not merely suffering present dangers and hardships in the hope of future gains, but that the road itself is a pleasant journey.

Chapter XII, beginning the list of the special blessings, deals with the providence of God, and differs from the concept expressed in Chapter III, because Granada now refers to temporal blessings. These blessings are rewards for the good to encourage them to persevere in the path to virtue, coupled with threats that harm may come to the wicked. Examples of this providential care are shelter from the heat of summer, succor in time of danger, aid in time of falling, and lifting of the spirits in time of discouragement. While good examples of providential care, these considerations do not argue conclusively for the pragmatic value of being good since even the wicked might be able to enjoy such blessings. One method which Granada uses for suggesting the diversity of providential care is to recall the names used for God which express this concern: Father, King, Eagle, Shepherd, Bridegroom, and others. One recalls the major work of Fray Luis de León, *De los nombres de Cristo* *(Of the Names of Christ)*. As is so often the case, our Fray Luis asks the sinner to contemplate the emptiness of life without God's providential care.

Chapter XIII treats of the second reward of virtue, the privilege of enjoying the grace of the Holy Spirit. Fray Luis gives two definitions of divine grace. The first, he says, is from the theologians. "Grace is a participation of Divine Nature, that is of the sanctity, goodness, purity, and nobility of God, by means of which man dismisses from himself the baseness and villainy which come to him from Adam, and [man] makes himself a participant in sanctity and divine nobility, divesting himself of his own nature and clothing himself in Christ." The second, which he says is from the saints (presumably the mystics), presents the definition of grace in the form of an analogy. Grace and the soul become like fire and iron respectively. Iron, placed in the fire, remains iron but takes on the aspects of fire.

Chapter XIV identifies the third privilege of virtue as the supernatural knowledge and light which God gives to those worthy of it. Highlighting this chapter is an analogy which concerns animal instincts and man. If God gives animals instincts to protect them by telling them which foods to eat and which to avoid, should we not expect Him to guide men in the right way? This divine illumination is a help to our understanding just as grace influences our wills. Granada makes clear that the purpose of divine guidance of our understanding is not for knowledge for its own sake, but for action as a result of knowledge.

In Chapter XV we find that the fourth privilege of virtue lies in the consolations of the Holy Spirit given to the good. Granada apparently feels that this is a different privilege from the grace of the Holy Spirit discussed in Chapter XIII. Just as in almost every chapter he finds an interesting analogy or comparison, so here he compares these consolations to wine. The person who drinks wine soon seems to partake of the nature of wine. The person intoxicated by the Holy Spirit will likewise seem to take on the nature of the Holy Spirit. A less startling example from the same chapter is found in the analogy of water over a flame (steam) which loses its heaviness and takes on the gaseous lightness of fire.

Chapter XVI lists as the fifth privilege the joy of a good conscience and, conversely, the avoidance of the suffering of remorse. Conscience is treated as a natural gift. Even those who are not Christians have a conscience to guide them in moral decisions. Granada quotes one philosopher as saying, "even if I knew that the gods would forgive me and that men would not know about it, I would not dare commit a sin simply because of the ugliness of it." He quotes St. Isidore as saying that a man can flee from anything but himself. With no violation of orthodox belief, Granada proposes that God helps virtuous non-Christians, at least to the extent of assisting them in their earthly existence. Granada had quite a feeling of rapport with thoughtful pagans of classic times, especially with Cicero and the Stoics.

Chapter XVII gives us the sixth privilege of virtue, the confidence and hope in divine mercy. This confidence comes from doing virtuous things, not from passively accepting the blessing. Fray Luis dwells mainly on the tribulations of those who mistakenly place their confidence elsewhere and find misery as a consequence. The seventh privilege of virtue, we are informed in Chapter XVIII, is the true freedom which the good possess, contrasted with the misery of those who lack that freedom. Service to the Lord is perfect freedom. Granada illustrates with a graphic allegory. He asks us to picture a man married to a woman who embodies all noble and beautiful qualities. This couple has a servant, a wicked mulatto woman who bewitches the husband, makes the wife a servant, and replaces her in her husband's love. This woman is, allegorically, human flesh, which can replace the virtuous wife who represents the human spirit. For many in the latter part of the twentieth century, Fray Luis has here sinned blatantly as a racist and a sexist, but I doubt that his contemporaries chided him for it. Certainly the allegorical lesson conveyed what he was stressing. Much of the thought of this chapter concerns being a slave to sin. Granada is emphatic in asserting that sin cannot enslave man's free will. Sin often weakens will to the point that it is enslaved temporarily, but the possibility of overthrowing the tyrant of sin is always there.

A kind of corollary of freedom is peace and interior quiet, the theme of Chapter XIX. Granada points out three aspects of that peace: our relationship with others, with God, and with ourselves. He observes that finding peace within ourselves is a problem which should surprise no one, since each man is really two men, a man of passion and a man of reason, each constantly opposing the other. Most of this chapter is devoted to the contrast between the internal strife of the wicked and the inner peace which the virtuous enjoy.

Chapter XX affirms that the ninth privilege of virtue is that God heeds the prayers of the good: "When we pray, although we may not see anyone, nor anyone respond to us, we do not speak to the walls, nor do we lash out at the air, but God is there listening to us and attending to our prayers, showing compassion for our needs, and making available to us the remedy if it is a remedy that is fitting."[5] He reminds us that in the Gospels we read, "ask and you shall receive; seek and you shall find; knock and it shall be opened to you." These and other promises that prayers will be answered are followed by examples of the testimony of saints whose prayers were answered. On the other hand, prayers must be offered in the right spirit. Granada warns the reader that if the spirit of the prayer is not that of contriteness of heart or if it is offered in a perfunctory manner it may be ignored. He cites St. Cyprian as saying that a petition is not effective if the prayer is sterile. He concludes the chapter optimistically for the weak by saying that sometimes even the prayers of the undeserving may be answered, since prayer may be a means by which the wicked are brought to God, as He in His mercy sometimes grants their petitions.

Chapter XXI presents the tenth privilege of virtue, the divine aid given to those suffering tribulation. Granada points out that all must suffer tribulation, but that when God allows tribulations to come to man, He measures them carefully to be sure that they are not excessive for the soul who is to receive them. Fray Luis leaves us with the impression that he considers that the tribulations which God permits are themselves a blessing, since virtue is honed upon them. The main point, of course, is that the strength which God gives the virtuous man to bear suffering and sorrow enables him to take tribulation in stride, while such problems vex and frustrate those who, by not living a life of virtue, lack the strength to face them. Perhaps God may give a man more tribulation than he can handle, but not if this man seeks the path of virtue. Fray Luis cites Chrysostom for a graphic symbol of this point: "The same fire which purifies gold, burns wood."[6]

The eleventh privilege of virtue is taken up in Chapter XXII, and concerns God's help in the temporal problems that men constantly encounter. This advantage is explicated by Fray Luis almost with reluctance, since the well-being of the spirit is much more important than that of the flesh. He does, however, wish to appeal to all sinners, including those interested in the quality of material things. He notes that the Jews are likely to be in this group. For an example of the blessings, he refers to Matthew 6 where we can read such things as "consider the fowls of the air: they sow not, neither do they reap, nor gather into barns, yet our Heavenly Father feedeth them. Are ye not much better than they?" This reference to the Jews is unusual for Granada. Whether he was following traditional gossip about the assumed materialism of the Jews or forming a personal opinion of Jews he had known is not at all clear.

Chapter XXIII gives us the twelfth privilege of virtue, a quiet and happy death. Many ideas expressed here are similar to thoughts in Chapter VII, but here the rewards of virtue are considered rather than the call to virtue. To give added emphasis, Granada reproduces several examples from St. Gregory's writings about blessed deaths. These include a brief but fairly complete biography of each person receiving a miraculous visitation at death. Granada speaks of these miracles as a reward gratuitously offered to some very virtuous people, not as a reward that a person might actively seek. It seems that the implication is that the average person who is trying to live a good life would find, not a miracle at death, but at least a tranquility of conscience. The idea of a supernatural visit at death with those in the wake aware of the miracle was of special importance during the Middle Ages and lingered in the sixteenth century despite Erasmus's opposition to attaching importance to such reports. We should recall that El Greco, a younger contemporary of Granada, painted the famous *Burial of Count Orgaz* with its visitation to the dying count by St. Augustine and St. Stephen.

The final pages of this chapter offer a recapitulation of the twelve privileges of virtue, compared to the twelve months of the year, and followed by a plea to the reader that he not consider the virtue to be found in Granada's own book in anything more than a human sense, but rather pray to God for the experience and use of the twelve God-given virtues.

VI *Book I, Part III: A Rebuttal*

The third part of Book I is devoted to Granada's responses to those who understand the nature of the life of virtue and who are ready to acknowledge their need for converting to such a life, but for various reasons, are not prepared to act immediately. Chapter XXIV discusses the first such persons, the simple procrastinators. The source of the problem, as Granada sees it, is a severe misinterpretation of the nature of God's mercy. According to the procrastinator's reasoning, in the process of man's salvation, if the main element is our redemption through Christ's sacrifice on the Cross and man's part is simply to accept it, is there any reason for rushing into repentance? Should not a man wait for what he himself considers a propitious time for repentance and for changing his ways?

Granada reacts with his usual manner of marshaling as many bits of logic as he can to defeat such an idea. In the first place, how does one know how long he will live? It surely would be bad if a man who intended to repent should die before doing so. But granting, for the sake of discussion, says Fray Luis, that a man might reasonably expect to live a long life, should he not strive to repent and to begin his life of virtue immediately? Changing one's habits is difficult. The longer they are ingrained, the more difficult they are to change: further bad habits may be started meanwhile. As an analogy for the reasoning of postponing repentance, Granada takes the case of a gatherer of firewood who gathered more than he could carry home.

His remedy was to seek more and more firewood, making his burden, already too much for him, even heavier. Absurd? Yes, but no more so than that of the man with more sins than he can overcome, who wants to add even more before he changes his way of life. As a further analogy of the way sin takes hold, Granada considers the example of Lazarus, raised by Christ from the dead after four days. Citing St. Augustine for the allegory, he says that the first day in the tomb of sin was the temptation *(deleite)*, the second, the consent, the third was the act *(la obra)*, and the fourth, the habit. At this point, only the special intervention of the Savior could remove the person concerned from permanent death in sin.

Numerous moving statements by saints and stoics attest to the idea that it is wrong to postpone repentance, because it runs counter to reason to add to the debt one owes the Redeemer. Putting off penitence until old age suggests that one would simply wait until he had nothing better to do, or until the temptation to sin was no longer strong, and then would repent. Granada tries hard to persuade the reader to show some virtue on his own initiative and not to depend entirely upon the mercy of God.

The importance of this consideration for the well-being of a Christian, particularly the reality of the problem of postponed repentance, is extremely well illustrated by two Golden-Age writers: Lope de Vega and Tirso de Molina. In the case of Lope, it was personal. In one of his most moving sonnets, Lope speaks of his own desire for repentance. Repeatedly he tells God that he will repent, tomorrow, while the next day, he is still saying, "tomorrow." Tirso expresses the theme in his best-known play, *El Burlador de Sevilla (The Deceiver of Seville)*. The servant, Catalinón, repeatedly warns his master, Don Juan Tenorio, that a day of reckoning is approaching, but Don Juan is confident that he can wait until he is ready. He goes to Hell before the audience and, too tardily having inquired about last-minute repentance, he is told that it is too late.

After the chapter on procrastination one would expect the next chapter to have a different theme, but actually it is more an intensification of the previous one. In Chapter XXV Granada asks, "What of those who wait up to the threshold of death to repent?" We may ask, "has he not already answered that one, almost trampling it to earth with the force of his logic?" His answer is that it should be, but not necessarily so. Granada's sources for the commentary on this question are the testimony of the holy fathers, the learned theologians (especially Scotus), and the Bible itself. He asks whether last-minute repentance is genuine? Would not such a man, if he should have a miraculous recovery, perhaps lose his fear of punishment and return to his evil ways? Even if repentance is sincere, he might not have the opportunity to try to right any wrongs that he might be expected to correct. In the midst of this discussion Granada realizes that he is becoming verbose: "It seems to me that I am spending a lot of time on such an obvious thing, but what can I do, if even with all of this, I see a large part of the world covering itself with this cloak?"

Fray Luis is finally ready to bring up the subject of the thief on the cross. Jesus promised the thief immediate salvation for his timely repentance. Can others not do the same? Granada's answer is, first, that it was a genuine and dramatic expression of faith at a time when even Christ's disciples were denying Him. Second, it was an extraordinary event, not intended to be a general rule for men to be guided by. It is true indeed that, if a man has waited until the last moment to repent, he should take advantage of his last chance, but it is perilous to wait deliberately for that moment to come.

In Chapter XXVI, Fray Luis speaks to those who continue in their sins, resting their hope in divine mercy. The idea of taking advantage of God's mercy in this way sounds so basically and grossly unjust to Granada that he expresses himself with unaccustomed severity. Quoting St. Bernard, he says that the two feet of God are justice and mercy. It is obvious that he feels in this instance that God will lean to the side of justice. Granada divides examples of the working of God's justice into two areas: the witness of Holy Scripture and the witness of this world. Naturally, he reveals his own passion at the thought that creatures, both callous and smug, might be able to take advantage of God's mercy without genuine repentance, but Granada doesn't lose his perspective. He does not want to despise these people; he wants to convert them.

The reader would naturally expect a change of tone in Chapter XXVII, which presents arguments against those who excuse themselves from immediate repentance because the road to virtue is too harsh and difficult. While the tone does change, Granada is still impatient. He reminds the reader that he is not abandoned to his own devices in this road to virtue, for God will help him. If the fearful person realizes that some people experience joy in following

God's commandments, things will not seem so difficult to him. Granada gives us the feeling that he is addressing the lazy rather than the timid at this point. Yet his natural mildness gradually reasserts itself. In a section of this chapter devoted to the assistance that love lends, he uses the example of a mother and baby. The care of this baby would be a very difficult task if the mother were not sustained by love.

If the light of reason is on the side of the good, and blind passion on the side of the wicked, the path of the good is actually easier to follow. Granada finishes the chapter by quoting at some length the testimony of two saints who found that after their conversion the path of virtue was unexpectedly easy because of the operation in their hearts of God's Grace. These witnesses were Cyprian and Augustine.

In Chapter XXVIII, Fray Luis warns that the path to virtue may be blocked to those who love the things of the world. He believes that the Christian will find worldly happiness deceptive for six reasons, each of which provides the title for a subchapter. The happiness of this earthly life must be compared to that of eternal life. How brief would even two hundred years be! (Two hundred years is taken as an absolute maximum for mortal life.) Our mortal life is like a dream, since it passes so quickly.[7] The happiness of this world is combined with its miseries; some of these are shared by those who seek virtue, since they are the product of mortality, but others are not, since they are the fruit of wickedness. The world is full of snares and dangers, of blindnesses and darkness, and of many sins. Finally, it is full of deception. Happiness is not as real as it appears to be. Hope is the only thing that the worldly have as an advantage over Hell. Fray Luis qualifies this by saying that at least that is the way St. Bernard looks at it. Granada seems to sense that he may be exaggerating.

Fray Luis does not formally define worldliness to distinguish his concept from things of the world which have no inherent quality of evil. Elsewhere he shows what a blessed place is this world that God has created. Therefore, in total context, it is obvious that Granada is not morbid about this earthly existence, nor does he look with undue scorn upon things that belong to a normal earthly existence.

Chapter XXIX provides a brief summary for Book I. Its unifying thesis is that the path of virtue is made worthwhile, joyful, and easy for those who trust in God and wish to follow Him.

VII   *Book II, Part I: Overcoming Sin*

The second Book of the *Sinner's Guide* assumes that the points
covered in Book I have been accepted. The sinner is now
thoroughly convinced that the path of virtue is desirable and attain-
able. Book II will offer thoughts for sustaining virtue once the pil-
grimage is undertaken. Two brief chapters outline Granada's presuppositions. These are recognition of the importance of this undertaking and willingness to devote the heart entirely to it. These two
chapters function as a preamble. Chapter III is written as an introduction to the subject matter of Book II, Part I. Each subsequent
chapter will treat one of the seven deadly sins: pride, avarice, lust,
envy, gluttony, anger, and sloth. There are three additional chapters: one in which Fray Luis describes what he calls sins related to
the seven major ones, a chapter on remedies against venial sins, and
a chapter of miscellaneous thoughts on all sins.

The main points of Chapter III are that the Christian should have
a very firm determination never to commit a major sin, and that the
avoidance of temptation requires more attention to the understanding of sin and its disguises than it does to weapons for fighting it or
feet for escaping from it.

Chapter IV, which gives suggestions for fighting pride, begins
with a classification of sins. All sin emanates from self-love. This love
engenders three other loves: the sensual pleasures, possessions, and
honor. Excessive love of sensual pleasures is manifested in the sins
of lust, gluttony, and sloth; love of possessions stimulates avarice,
and love of honor, pride. Anger and envy serve all the other sins.
Pride is considered the queen of the vices. A proud man should first
consider that pride caused the fall from Heaven of Lucifer. He
dropped from the status of the greatest of the angels to the worst of
the demons. The proud person should contemplate the humility of
Christ in contrast to his own misplaced pride. Pride pleases no one.
God humbles the proud and raises the meek. Naturally, the humble
person hates the proud one. Other proud people see rivals. Finally,
a proud person can not really satisfy himself. Pride in achievement
soon draws attention to the pride rather than to the achievement.

The natural remedy is to seek humility, trying to see the virtue in
others' accomplishments. True humility is usually found in showing
patience when one is suffering. A proud person should not dress
beyond his station. Conversely, he should not dress beneath his

station, for conspicuous humility is inverted pride. There is nothing great in being humble when what one has done is small, so a person should beware of taking pride in his humility.

In Chapter V Granada defines avarice in three parts: excessive greed leading to robbery, covetousness of another's possessions, and excessive love of one's own wealth. The first consideration of the man fighting avarice is to consider the poor and humble life of Christ. Granada reminds us that no man can serve two masters, God and wealth. He further advises that wealth is not acquired without work, preserved without worry, or lost without pain. Love of wealth torments more with desire than it delights with its use. Acquiring wealth often causes offenses against God. Consider the example of Judas who betrayed Christ for wealth. Furthermore, the acquisition of wealth is self-defeating, since the more one tries to accumulate wealth the more dissatisfied he is with what he has. The wealthy man will find at death that his treasures are a hindrance. One will simply have more things to account for before God.

God provided man with what is necessary for his bodily needs, and the man who accumulates more than he needs robs the poor of what God wanted them to have. It is not wealth itself that causes the sin of avarice; it is the love of it. As a corollary, the poor are not blessed for being poor but for patience in enduring what they must and for not coveting what others have.

Chapter VI was written to help the Christian fight the temptations to lust. Granada considers lust especially evil, since it befouls the spirit which Christ cleansed with His blood and also befouls the body which is the temple of the Holy Spirit. The temptation to lust is strong, but the pleasures are fleeting. One's reputation is easily ruined, diseases and premature aging often accompany the lustful. Lust can afflict great men—David succumbed to lust and as a result committed homicide, scandal, and adultery.

Granada warns men to beware of the company of women: hearing them attracts men, speaking with them influences men, touching them stimulates, and everything about them is a snare. Fray Luis then presents two stories taken from the *Dialogues* of St. Gregory. In the first story, a priest, with a great fear of God, had a virtuous washerwoman. He loved her as if she were a sister but avoided her as if she were an enemy. He had a serious illness and she was leaning over him to see if he was still breathing. He ordered her away angrily and went immediately to his grave, joyfully since he had overcome temptation. In the second story, Bishop Andrew had a virtuous woman living in his house. He tried to be careful about his relationship to her, but a demon tempted him and he noticed her face and later gave her a pat on the back. Meanwhile, a Jew was seeking domicile in a pagan temple, first crossing himself as he had seen Christians do. He accidentally eavesdropped upon a meeting of devils bragging about the bishop's plight. He warned the bishop, who prayed to St. Andrew, and after dismissing the woman, was tempted no more, while the Jew was converted.

Granada does not offer advice to women tempted by lust. They can, of course, get some ideas on proper precautions from what he says to the men. It is obvious that Granada does not consider lust a sin confined to wicked men. The examples from St. Gregory indicate that even two virtuous people, in spite of taking extraordinary precautions, are in danger of the temptation to lust. Granada's remedy is even greater vigilance and fervent prayer. These examples taken from St. Gregory and the one earlier from St. Bernard seem fanatical, not only in a twentieth-century context but from the standpoint of Granada's usual perspective as well. He has a natural tendency, when preaching against lust, to make his cases strong, but another factor operating here is his respect for authority. If St. Gregory said it, it must be true.

Chapter VII is directed against envy. Numerous examples of envy mentioned in the Bible are cited: Cain's envy of Abel, Saul's envy of David, and Aaron's envy of Moses. Envy, Granada tells us, is found in courts, palaces, and among wealthy people, and even in universities. One unusual quality of envy cited is that the one guilty of envy punishes himself.[8] To curb envy one may try to curb ambition. Even if the person who is the cause of envy be wicked, one should not hate him but rather hate the source, as a doctor hates illness but not the sick one.

Chapter VIII helps to guard against gluttony. Granada frequently reminds the reader, as he does here, that it is important for the intellect to control the passions, for the soul not to yield to the demands of the body. He cites the example of Lazarus, the beggar, now resting in Abraham's bosom, while the gluttonous rich man now suffers the torments of the damned.

Fray Luis here inserts a curious note. He states that death as man's universal punishment arose from gluttony. He evidently is referring to original sin, the tasting of the forbidden fruit. Since his explanations normally take full advantage of analogy, allegory, and symbolism, one may be puzzled by his literalness here. The specific sin of Adam and Eve was disobedience, and if Eve is given the primary blame for the sin, it must stem from her curiosity, not her gluttony. If the sin of the taking of the forbidden fruit can come under one of the classic seven deadly sins, it should presumably come under pride. It may be concluded that Granada is more interested in having one eat less than he is in providing the proper classification of sins for the record.

The one who tends to lose his temper should study Chapter IX carefully. Fray Luis reminds us that animals, many of them with offensive weapons given to them by God's providence, decline to use them for simple vengeance upon their own kind, but save them for their natural enemies. Granada suggests reciting the Lord's Prayer or the alphabet when one feels temper rising—anything to give himself a little time to combat the impulse to violence. He compares anger to wine, since both can affect the rational processes.

The last of the seven deadly sins, sloth, is the subject of Chapter X. Those who lack diligence should think first of how hard Christ worked for man, of how diligent the apostles and other early Christians were, and then consider the various forces and creatures of nature that perform their functions regularly. The lazy person will need to remember that he will not gain energy as he grows older. Finally, he should bear in mind that if he has real diligence, when tempted by sloth, he will not only be able to resist temptation but he will substitute a virtue for it.

Chapter XI covers two sins not normally included with the seven just cited. These are, taking God's name in vain and gossiping about one's neighbors. Taking God's name in vain has two aspects. One is simple profanity. This is not a mortal sin, simply a bad habit, perhaps a manifestation of anger. But if it is a deliberate oath involving a falsehood, then Granada labels it a mortal sin, an offense committed directly against God. Listening to gossip is almost as bad as telling it. It is relatively harmless unless it descends to slander, but this is very easy to do. Very similar is making judgments when one may not have the facts to judge properly or when one may have prejudices. Similarly, Chapter XII discusses venial sins. Granada is not specific about them but calls attention to their number, likely to be large, and especially to their possible weakening of the soul, making it less able to resist major temptations. Venial sins may be small manifestations of the major ones: peeves, instead of full-blown anger, idle thoughts, a little too much sleep, or similar peccadillos.

Chapter XIII, the last chapter in Book II, Part I, presents a series of dialogues between a vice and its opposing virtue. Granada states that he is quoting St. Augustine and then notes that some authorities have attributed these quotations to Pope St. Leo. As an example of this dialogue:

Lust says, "why do you not enjoy now your delights and pleasures, since you do not know what is destined for you? It is not right that you waste this good time because you don't know how soon it will pass away. Because if God didn't want men to enjoy these pleasures He would not have created men and women in the beginning." Chastity responds, "I don't want you to pretend that you do not know what is destined for you after this life. Because if you live cleanly and purely you will have endless pleasure and joy, and if dishonestly [lustfully] you will be taken to eternal torments and the more that you feel that time is passing lightly, the more important it is to you to live purely, because the hour of pleasure is very miserable when one loses life that lasts forever."[9]

VIII   *Book II Part II: The Practice of Virtue*

The organization of Book II, Part II is somewhat more complex than that of the previous divisions of the *Sinner's Guide*. This part treats the practice of the virtues. Chapter XIV, a very short chapter, is an introduction that tells the reader that the virtues will be discussed under three headings: man's duty to God, to his neighbor, and to himself. The next three chapters take these considerations in reverse order. Chapter XVIII describes the various obligations of people according to their stations in life. Following this, in Chapters XIX–XXII, come four reminders (*avisos*) connected with the maintenance of the virtues. With these four reminders the *Sinner's Guide* ends.

Chapter XV, a long chapter, contains Granada's advice to the virtue-seeker as to his duty to himself. Fray Luis begins by pointing out that the external man and internal self should be in harmony. Granada then proceeds, in what he considers ascending order, to deal with the reformation of the body. First, one should be moderate in food and drink. Not only should one consume sparingly, he should not dwell upon the pleasures of consumption. He should be especially careful of wine, for chastity trembles in its presence, and seldom is a secret safe where wine is queen.

If a person is sensuous he should try not only to avoid the sins of the senses but to curb also his enjoyment of legitimate things, such as looking upon rich tapestry, since the mind thus occupied can scarcely concentrate upon spiritual things. Pleasures of the sense of smell, such as that given by perfume, are for women, and evil ones at that, so men should certainly shun these. One should be careful with his tongue. He is not admonished especially to be silent but rather to be careful of what he says—when, where, and in whose company. All of the passions should be kept under control.

Granada now turns to higher considerations: the reformation of the will, the imagination, and the understanding. For the will, one should seek "humility of heart, poverty of spirit, and a holy hatred of oneself." This does not mean that man should become bored with his life; rather, he should follow the example of the saints in their mortification of the flesh. The task of the control of the imagination lies mainly in struggling to keep alert for work to be done and to retain concentration during prayer. As Fray Luis addresses himself to the topic of the reformation of the understanding, he urges prudence and gives a rather extended definition of it. An example of prudence is knowing how to deal with others, to endure others' faults, to know oneself, and not to trust everyone (other examples follow). A special subchapter on prudence in business matters includes the following: commending all our dealings to God, examining our affairs carefully, not acting hastily, watching out for the four "stepmothers": haste, passion, obstinacy, and vanity. One should seek to profit from one's mistakes as well as one's successes and those of others. Finally, one should seek humility, not that of a weak, unstable character, but the humility that comes from prayer.

Chapter XVI, surprisingly short and fitted in between two long chapters, deals with man's duty to his neighbor. The Spanish word used here is *prójimo,* which does not quite convey the pleasant connotations of neighbor, but simply the idea of fellowman. Thus a feeling of love toward such a person would seem to require a more virtuous attitude than one might otherwise expect. Granada points out how vain are man's efforts to appease God if this love for others is not in his heart. He presents five words which accompany love and are manifestations and degrees of love: advise, aid, suffer, forgive, and edify. Love seems to him incomplete if any one of these is missing. Perhaps one cannot truly edify others until he has shown the other forms of loving. Fray Luis also considers the negative aspects of man's duty to his neighbor. He must not judge, speak evil, nor vex his neighbor in his property, honor, or wife. He must not scandalize him with injurious or discourteous words, and especially should avoid bad examples and advice. As a climax to the chapter, one is asked to imagine that his acts and attitudes are directed toward Christ instead of toward his fellowman.

Chapter XVII deals with man's duty to God. For our convenience Granada tells us at the beginning that he will treat nine points—nine virtues necessary for man to acquire in order to fulfill his duty to God. These are love, fear and reverence, confidence, zeal for divine honor, purity of intention in God's service, prayer and recourse to God for all our needs, gratitude for his blessings, obedience and conformity to His will, and humility and patience in all trials that He sends us.

The last two are treated somewhat more extensively than the others. Granada tells us that there are four degrees of obedience: to obey God's commands, to follow His advice, to be influenced by His inspiration, and for the most virtuous, to surrender the will completely to God; the will should be as soft wax in God's hands. As for patience in suffering, there are also degrees: one may accept adversity with patience, desire it for the love of Christ, and rejoice in it for the same reason. Fray Luis makes it clear that rejoicing in tribulation goes beyond what Christ requires of anyone. In one of his many comparisons, he suggests that a person may ford a river directly or he may fight the current to be sure that he is not too far downstream when he reaches the other side. Thus an extra effort ensures some margin for the troubles one may encounter. By way of a summary of the last three chapters, Granada suggests that to serve ourselves we need the heart of a judge; to serve others, the heart of a mother; to serve God, the heart of a son.

In Chapter XVIII, Granada discusses the duties that correspond to social status. A prelate has a grave responsibility for those in his charge. A subject has the responsibility of obedience to his prelate as if it were to God Himself. Similar advice is given to families with their relationships of father and son, husband and wife, master and servant. The one in charge is expected to recognize and shoulder his responsibilities. Granada considers here neither the subject of tyranny nor that of rebellion. The subordinate is expected to assume that he can trust the one in charge and should obey without question.

In Chapter XIX, Fray Luis gives us the first synthesis of the preceding catalog of virtues and methods of obtaining them. The most important virtues, he says, are the theological ones (faith, hope, and charity) and, along with them, the other interior or spiritual virtues. Those which are more visible and exterior, such as fasting, silence, various acts of attending mass, pilgrimages, sermons, and divine offices, are to be considered as secondary, even though significant and essential. Fray Luis reminds us that if we can bear in mind this relativity of importance in virtue we can avoid two extremes: one is that of the Pharisees, who exaggerate the importance of overt acts and ostentatious piety even though the interior spirit may be lacking; at the same time, we must avoid the heretics who say that these observances simply are not necessary.

Granada seldom worries about the Protestants. When he does, it is natural that he should call them heretics. What is surprising is that their presumed deviations from the virtuous life are, in Granada's view, apparently lesser in nature than those of the Pharisees, who, according to this view, would be the superorthodox Catholics who behave as though a feast of ritual can hide a famine of the spirit. Granada proves here, as on so many other occasions, that his is a genuinely eclectic spirit. There is no trace of heterodoxy in him, but his natural feeling is for the preservation of the spirit of reform. He is thus far closer to the views of Erasmus than might appear at first glance.

Chapter XX presents amplification of the synthesis begun in the preceding chapter. Fray Luis describes four principles bearing upon application of the virtues to daily living. First, the Christian is to observe all essential virtues, those described as exterior as well as those described as interior. Second, the virtues are not of equal importance, since the interior ones are more basic. Third, there may be times in which one is forced to choose between the application of two virtues, at which time he should postpone the lesser. Fourth, there is false virtue as well as true. The fourth point is the one most fully treated. The exterior virtues are most obvious to the public. The person who pretends to be virtuous, exaggerates the visible signs and becomes a hyprocrite. There are two kinds of hypocrites: those aware of their hypocrisy and those who deceive themselves. Virtue can be hot, cold, or tepid. The worst of these is tepid, since it usually represents a warming of the exterior virtues without a consequent warming of the interior ones. As Granada provides examples from the Bible and from other ancient sources to illustrate these principles, he reminds us that human nature does not change and so these principles do not become obsolete. This chapter seems to reinforce the idea that Granada was more concerned with the interior reform of men's hearts than with the danger of heresy emanating from rival religious sects. I strongly suspect that this was his natural inclination. If so, it was obviously bolstered by the knowledge that the people who would read or listen to a reading of his book were not those likely to fall under the influence of Luther, Calvin, or Zwingli. This spirit, however, was not the prevailing one at the Council of Trent.

After it has been repeatedly shown that one should consider all kinds of virtues necessary for the good life, Fray Luis tells us in Chapter XXI that it is natural and proper to specialize. In the exercise of our talents and of our inclinations, we should try to do well what we do best. These specializations proceed from natural differences and also from differences in grace. The thrust of Granada's lesson here, however, is that we not judge one another. He apparently fears that a man will have a tendency to look upon his own specialization as most important and thus scorn those who serve God differently. For example, one who finds meditation meaningful should not disdain another who seeks to serve God mainly by good works. Thus, even while attempting to serve God, one may be tempted to measure himself against others, to the detriment of that harmonious diversity which is God's plan.

Chapter XXII suggests a general rule to overcome the bewilderment that one may feel from listening to so many specific exhortations and warnings: be vigilant. Granada seems to say, "In other words be careful and be thorough." With Seneca he exhorts a person to seek a good model to follow. He then suggests that a person act as if this might be his last day on earth, and that especially he should be aware that he is performing in the presence of God.

Chapter XXIII, the last chapter in the *Sinner's Guide*, asks where to find the strength of will to persevere in a life of virtue after having been shown the way. One's strength comes from the Lord, but Granada offers a practical warning in this connection. Those who have followed some spiritual guides may think that God will make things easy for them. The way, however, is often difficult. One should take as his inspiration the martyrs who suffered for righteousness' sake and from Christ on the Cross. The final exhortation is a biblical quotation. "If any man would come after me, let him take up his cross and follow me."[10]

The *Sinner's Guide* is not quite the complete encyclopedia for virtue. Several times Fray Luis refers to his *Memorial of the Christian Life*. The person interested in getting help in making his prayer life more meaningful should certainly turn there in preference to the *Sinner's Guide*. The non-Christian, and especially any one who does not accept any supernatural religious tenets, is unlikely to be convinced by Granada's manner of reasoning. The typical Spanish Christian, however, who has no epistemological preoccupations and whose prayers are likely to be more ritualistic than emotional, should find this guide to be all that he needs to show him the path to virtue and help him to stay on it. This kind of person needed a book that was more optimistic than Kempis' *Imitation of Christ*, but which spoke with equal simplicity, forthrightness, and perseverance. The more scholarly or more mystical reader should seek other references.

CHAPTER 4

Prayer and Mysticism

I The Source Materials

IN this Chapter we will consider three different books by Granada, the *Libro de la oración y meditación* (*Book of Prayer and Meditation*), the *Memorial de la vida cristiana* (*Memorial of the Christian Life*), and the *Adiciones al memorial de la vida cristiana* (*Additions to the Memorial of the Christian Life*). We will not attempt a part-by-part or chapter-by-chapter analysis of these works but will use them as references for the general analysis of Granada's guidance on prayer and mysticism. Since Granada himself did not write books or treatises specifically devoted to the subject of mysticism, we must try to organize his thoughts on mysticism which form an extension of his thoughts on prayer.

The Book of Prayer and Meditation is divided into three parts. The parts are in turn divided into chapters of very unequal length, the longest of which has forty-two subchapters. The first part is the heart of the work. In several introductory chapters, Granada deals with the five parts of prayer (which we will define and consider in some detail later), followed by seven admonitions related to these five parts. Following these are fourteen meditations, one for each day in the week, evening and morning. The final chapter in Part I offers a description of six aspects of the passion of Christ to use for meditation. The first part has thus answered the need for material for meditation and for advice concerning how to do it. The second part is planned to help man increase his fervor for prayer. It deals with those things which aid or impede a spirit of devotion to Christ. The third part, almost an appendix, has three treatises, the first on prayer, the second on fasting, and the third on almsgiving.

The Memorial of the Christian Life is divided into seven treatises: first, an exhortation to righteous living; second, penitence and confession; third, preparation for communion; fourth, avoidance of sin and acquisition of virtue; fifth, vocal prayer; sixth, mental prayer; and seventh, the love of God and perfection in Christian life. The first of these is the shortest, with a general tendency for the treatises to become longer as one approaches the end. *Additions to the Memorial to the Christian Life* consists of two long treatises, one on the love of God, the other a meditation on the life of Christ.

We propose in this chapter to summarize and analyze the material of the *Book of Prayer and Meditation* approximately in the order in which Granada presents it and to follow with an analysis of passages of the other two books relevant to prayer or the mystical experience. Some material of the two memorials will not be treated in this chapter as it duplicates matter contained in *Sinner's Guide.*

II Granada's Study of Prayer: The Meditations

According to Granada, a prayer, strictly speaking, is a petition that one makes to God, but Fray Luis prefers to deal with a broader definition, which calls prayer any lifting of the heart to God, including meditation and contemplation. Probably the most important assumption of Fray Luis in dealing with this subject is that the individual who wants help in learning to pray is one who wants to dedicate his life to God and to the pursuit of the life that God wants him to live. Therefore Granada does not try, as he did in *Sinner's Guide*, to convince people of the need to pray. The purpose of prayer is to have the one praying feel closer to God and to seek His will. Whether his reader is a member of a religious order does not matter as far as the relevance of the book is concerned. Granada assumes that the reader will devote considerable time to prayer, morning and evening, every day.

Fray Luis divides the subject of prayer into five parts or stages. The first of these is preparation. He assumes that the reader need not be told to seek a quiet time and place. He does not immediately indicate a proper position of the body for prayer, but later suggests that some prayer time be spent on the knees and some in other positions so that fatigue will not become an impediment to devotion. Granada's first consideration is that the reader recognize that the most important part of prayer is to ask for forgiveness of sins. Therefore one should consider those acts of the day which need to be confessed. He should not dwell on them too long or in too much detail in order that they not incite him to further evil. He should, as a part of his preparation, consider the greatness and majesty of God to induce proper humility. For evening prayer he should be thinking mainly of seeking forgiveness for the day's sins; for morning prayer he should seek help to avoid sin during the day. A falsely pious attitude should be avoided by concentrating on doing the will of God rather than seeking personal consolation. Granada suggests that certain vocal prayers, especially rhymed ones, precede meditation.

The second stage of prayer is reading that material which is to be the subject of meditation. This reading should not be hurried, because one must understand fully what he is to meditate upon. Nevertheless, it should not be too prolonged lest it take time away from the other phases of the prayer cycle. It can be prolonged to the extent necessary if a person is finding meditation difficult, but he must realize that this reading is only a substitute for prayer as rye or barley might be for wheat.

The third stage is meditation. Fray Luis says that there are two kinds of materials for meditation. One, such as the meditation upon the life and passion of Christ, is for the imagination. In context, this seems to refer to subjective, sentimental meditation. The other is intellectual meditation, as when we think of the blessings that we receive. The imagination used during meditation must be controlled and the mind prevented from wandering. In discussing meditation, Granada, as many others do, uses the word "recollected." The word specifically means that a person is withdrawn into himself. I believe that as Granada and others use the term, it means more than that. It implies that such a person has his consciousness collected and concentrated upon the subjects of meditation and that the imagination is disciplined and focused upon the intended image or subject matter. Nothing mundane is competing for the mind's attention.

The fourth part of prayer is thanksgiving. Granada suggests that this may be almost a continuation of the meditation so that the thread of devotion is not broken. The thanksgiving is not intended as expressing gratitude for material blessings but for the spiritual ones. Many of those enumerated at this point, such as creation, conservation, and redemption, are discussed at some length in the *Sinner's Guide*.

The final part of prayer is petition, which as Fray Luis has previously told us, is the essence of prayer by its more narrow definition.

A person should ask first for blessings to be bestowed upon his neighbor. For himself he should ask for forgiveness of his sins and for strength and virtue to help avoid sin in the future. Granada lists sixteen virtues in groups of four. The first four named are integration of the external and internal man, discretion and care in all that one does or says, restraint and circumspection with the tongue, and severity and austerity in treating oneself. The second and third of these virtues seem to overlap slightly. His second four are virtues which he says are somewhat derivative and subordinate; but he does not fully explain the nature of this derivation. These are: perfect obedience, mortification of self-will, strength for all work and difficulty, and scorn for oneself. Eventually Granada enumerates eight others: interior and exterior humility, poverty of spirit and body, patience in all adversities, purity of intention in all good works, firm faith in all that God says and promises, a secure hope in Him as true Father, love of God always burning in the heart, and justice in all deeds. Having listed these, Granada asks the petitioner to think briefly about each.

There may be some imperfections in the general logic of his listing of the sixteen items. For the fundamental purpose of getting the person into the right frame of mind for fruitful prayer, both the psychology and pedagogy seem excellent. As a transition between the discussion of the five parts of prayer and the meditations which are to follow, Granada next gives seven suggestions *(avisos)* as guidelines. First, if one is using Granada's series of meditations and a special subject presents itself which seems more timely, he should meditate upon it and postpone the regular series. Second, a person who meditates should avoid excessive speculation about his meditation. Intellectual understanding is important, but intellectual curiosity can become an impediment to devotion. Third—the reverse of the second—one should beware of an excessively emotional response. Granada senses that a melodramatic quality in meditation may reveal a lack of profundity, as though a person were trying to convince himself that he is praying. Fourth, one should employ a spirit of moderation in these exercises to assure continuity. Fifth, if a person is seeking spiritual consolation through these meditations he should not despair if the consolations are slow in coming. Sixth, if he receives some spiritual consolation, he should not rest at that point but continue his devotional exercises. Seventh, if a person receives a spiritual consolation, it should serve him as a stimulus in the further pursuit of virtue. Again, one may notice overlapping in the sixth and seventh suggestions.

I should like to add a few guidelines to those Granada has already mentioned and which seem helpful for following Granada's lead. First, the aim of meditation for him is to help the reader orient his life in the service of God. It is not an exercise primarily in learning or understanding. It is part of the five stages of prayer, a part subordinated to the whole, but not a stage in a mystical ascent. If through these meditations one seems to be receiving consolations, Granada would have this person show gratitude for such blessing, but also consider it an inspiration to seek a still more virtuous life as defined in the *Sinner's Guide*, rather than seeking the more intimate personal relationship that the mystical process implies.

Second, these meditations officially contain material for one week, but obviously it would take much longer to use all of them for meditative purposes. Granada himself says:

It is not required that at one time one consider all of God's blessings; it is enough to think about one, or two, or three if they are well considered and meditated upon; because meditation exercises are not to be viewed as piece work which is to be finished but as the maintenance for each day, and the more carefully they are considered and the better they are digested, the more they do for the health.[1]

Third, there are apparent inconsistencies which have their explanation in the nature of meditation. For example, at one moment Granada will ask his reader to consider what a wretched creature man is. While he is establishing a contrast between the sins of man and the perfections of God, he vilifies man again and again. At another moment, Granada will ask his reader to consider the providence of God. Now, what a wonderful creature man is, exalted above all other creatures of God! Thus, at times it is dangerous to quote Granada in these meditations, especially where he is commenting on how to approach them; but despite the danger of inconsistency or distortion of his real attitude, it is almost necessary to quote him to capture the style, flavor, and zeal of the meditations.

The evening series of meditations begins with Monday night as the meditator is asked to dwell upon his sins. How numerous and varied the sins are, how often they occur, how grave they are! How grieved God is to observe them! How one's own conscience accuses him! Then if the conscience is determined to assert itself, if the sinner becomes truly penitent, God's help is at hand.

For Tuesday night, the theme for meditation is how miserable the world is. Life is short, uncertain, fragile, inconstant, and deceptive; and finally, death itself is miserable. The "world" and the life of misery described are the world as it actually would exist if there were no godly and virtuous elements. Materialism, coveting of and searching for ephemeral things, wars fought over the possession of things that do not matter—these are the things to think about and try to correct.

Wednesday's thoughts are turned to death. This is, of course, death as it would be approached by one living in that sin deplored in the Monday meditation and suffering the worldly existence and strife mentioned on Tuesday. Stress is given, however, to the idea that even men known for their saintliness feared death, since to some degree they also were sinners. Somewhere in each meditation there is a word of hope for relief or for avoidance of the conditions described in the meditation.

Thursday night is the time for thinking about Judgment Day. This time Granada is referring to the final Judgment Day for the universe. He mentions the signs and portents in the Bible heralding this event. He pictures in awesome manner the thought of approaching the day of God's decision, for any man knows that if the decision is against him, it is because of often-repeated acts and thoughts of stubborn rebellion against the divine will.

On Friday, the subject of meditation is the tortures of Hell. The physical tortures that one suffers, the greater anguish of the spirit, the eternity and unrelieved quality of the suffering—all are considered at length and in detail, but Granada stresses most of all the separation from God, the sense of having lost what one could have enjoyed forever.

The person who feels the emotional impact of these meditations must experience relief at reaching the Saturday meditation. After dwelling upon sin, misery, death, judgment, and Hell, he is finally ready to contemplate the joys of Paradise. Here he is asked to look upon the beauty and vastness of Heaven, the wonderful company of the saints, the clear vision of God, the joy of the soul in the glorification of the body, and the fact that the blessings of Heaven are eternal. Here and elsewhere in these meditations, Granada refers to

the Bible whenever possible as proof of the accuracy and timeliness
of his assertions.

The meditation of Sunday night is upon the blessings that God has
bestowed and is ready to bestow upon man. These are creation,
preservation, redemption, calling, and the special blessings given to
individuals. After five nights of dwelling upon the miseries of an
existence without God's influence, one upon the nature of Heaven,
and one upon all that God has done and stands ready to do to lift
man from one existence to the other, the person who has thought
carefully about these things should certainly now wish to bend every
effort to forsake evil and cling to the life of virtue. Near the end,
Granada stops addressing the reader and turns his thoughts directly
to Christ and the Cross:

O severe cross, do not remain inert, soften your hardness a little, bend
your tall branches, lower for me such precious fruit that I may taste of it. O
cruel nails, leave those innocent feet and hands, come to my heart and
strike it for I am the one who sinned, and not He. O good Jesus what have I
done to you with so many pains, with nails, with death, with the Cross?[2]

Fray Luis is capable of moving men's hearts because his own has
been moved.

There is a rather significant difference in the nature of the evening and morning meditations. The former are seven separate meditations which together can be considered a treatise upon life with
sinful and worldly characteristics, featuring man's baseness, contrasted with the life of virtue, showing the wonderful qualities of
God and the rewards for following His way. It moves from the
pessimistic meditation upon sinful man to the optimistic meditation
of the joys of Heaven and the blessings of God. The morning meditations are a single unit, a commentary upon Christ's life from the
time of the Last Supper until Easter Morning, following mainly the
story as told in the last three chapters of the Gospel of Matthew. The
morning meditations, like the evening ones, are divided into seven
parts, but these divisions are more like stoppings places. For example, the Monday meditation includes Christ's foretelling of his betrayal, the washing of the disciples' feet, and the establishment of
the Holy Communion. Each event is worthy of commentary and
meditation, but their juxtaposition is merely chronological in the
Bible rather than logical.

Granada then has the familiar events continue serving meditation: the agony of Gethsemane culminating in Christ's arrest following Judas's betrayal of Him, Peter's denial of Christ, the hearings before the various judges and rulers (Annas, Caiaphas, Herod, and Pilate), the walk to Calvary, and the Crucifixion. For Saturday, he asks the reader to meditate upon Christ's death, imagining what is going on in the heart of His Mother, and of course, the Sunday meditation is upon the Resurrection. No other period in the life of Christ is so passionate. No other passage from the Bible is comparable. Nevertheless, Granada seems to keep a measured emotional quality, following his own advice about the balance between the emotional and intellectual. One gets the impression that the emotions expressed are those that Granada feels rather than emotions that he is trying to provoke.

Fray Luis suggests that Christ's death was for two purposes: to redeem the world through His sacrifice and to dramatize the act to try to influence emotionally the heart of the one He is trying to redeem. Consider the following examples:

Well do I see, my Lord, that these injuries were not necessary for my redemption; a single drop of your blood was enough for this. But they were very useful for you to declare to me the greatness of your love, and for you to throw chains of perpetual obligation around me, for you to confound the manifestations of my vanity and teach me through it the scorn for the world's glory.[3]

Granada is at his best in poignant contrast, normally that between human and divine qualities.

Be ashamed, o my soul looking to the Lord upon this Cross and notice that from it He preaches to you and warns you saying, "O man, for your sake I received a crown of thorns and in scorn of Me, do you wear a garland of flowers? For your sake I stretched out my hands on the Cross, and do you extend yours in pleasure and dancing? I did not quench my thirst for water while dying, and do you seek expensive food and wine? I was on the Cross and throughout my life was filled with dishonors and suffering, and do you waste all of your life in pursuit of honors and pleasures? I allowed my side to be opened to give you my heart, and do you have yours opened for vain and dangerous loves?"[4]

Since the morning meditations are taken from a section of the Bible, those who have access to the Bible can use them as a model for meditating upon other spiritual passages. If a passage seems appropriate for learning, the reader can meditate upon its meaning. If it is more appropriate for the emotional response, perhaps the reader has now learned how to draw from it those emotions which will inspire him to a new zeal for righteousness. Fray Luis did not consider the morning meditations as a mere example of how to meditate, but there remains the implication that the reader can now find his own further material for meditation.

In the final chapter of Part I Granada considers the passion of Jesus as a summary of the preceding meditation, calling it of the greatest importance. He sees this meditation upon Christ's passion as a unit, but he recognizes that the reader will not automatically see its unity and so tries to synthesize it. He invites the reader to consider especially six things: the greatness of the suffering of Christ so that one may show compassion for Him, the gravity of one's sins so as to abhor them, the loftiness of this blessing to be grateful for it, the excellence of divine Goodness to love it, the large number of the virtues of Christ which shine there so as to imitate them, and the convenience of this means that God has chosen for his redemption so that he may marvel at divine wisdom. A subchapter for each of the six is included to describe these points in detail. Granada's penchant for numbers is furthered here by numerous lists of thoughts in elaboration of the six main ones which we have listed. For example, in the elaboration of his first point, Granada lists five causes of Christ's suffering and twelve examples of it. For purposes of meditation this numbering system seems excellent; it should aid greatly in the concentration. For this book I think (and the reader should agree) that I have already provided enough numbered lists to read.

As we look back over Part I, it is obvious that Granada has directed his guide for prayer and meditation to those anxious to pray and to do so in the proper way. Unlike his approach in *Sinner's Guide*, he does not treat his reader with the delicacy accorded one who may easily forget his resolve. I see a paradox here, since only a relatively patient reader will meditate these long hours upon the subject of how evil and corrupt he is; the one really evil and corrupt will be too busy at his evil and corruption to heed Granada's words. One can see traces—including a few quotations—of the *Imitation of Christ*, which Granada translated sixteen years before publishing the *Book of Prayer and Meditation*. Neither author is angry toward the reader who is so vilified. Both include themselves in this vilification. If the one who meditates upon these pages comes with a contrite heart, he will probably not even notice how strong was the language used to describe his shortcomings. His soul will be full of gratitude for the Providence of God.

III *Granada's Study of Prayer: The Commentaries*

As we have seen, the first part of the *Book of Prayer and Meditation* is a practice book for meditation. The second part will deal with Granada's analysis of and teaching about problems of integrating the life of prayer with other aspects of living. The goal of Christian living should be to attain devotion. Granada does not give a concise definition of devotion, but perhaps we can understand his meaning by reflecting upon the thoughts presented in this part. Obviously for Granada, devotion is concentration upon doing the will of God, and the most important consideration is to develop and maintain control over one's thoughts and actions in order to be able to offer himself in God's service. The time spent in prayer must be harmonized with that accorded other religious duties such as observance of Sacraments and other church rites and with the performance of works of charity. Ultimately, prayer is not a goal but a means of acquiring the spirit of devotion. Granada is repeatedly concerned about achieving a balance among the demands placed upon the Christian's time and energy.

Fray Luis is constantly moving his reader's attention from considerations about prayer to other aspects of a Christian life. The heart must be kept in tune just as is a delicate musical instrument, and all paths to devotion must be explored to assure a harmonious life. The first step is mortification of the desires of the flesh. These desires must be stamped out; there is no compromise with them nor sublimation of them. Granada does offer two moderating ideas: one is his distinction between those things which are evil and those which, while not evil in themselves, are impediments to a life of devotion; second, there are suggestions for avoiding a spirit of fanaticism, especially the idea that the fanatic may confuse the means with the end or that he may fall into one sin while trying desperately to avoid its opposite. Nevertheless, the struggle against worldliness is intense and implacable.

Can the ascetic spirit harmonize with the mystical? The answer for Granada is yes, but his manner of reconciling the two may differ from that of most mystics. For Granada, meditation is within the reach of all. He claims that vocal and mental prayer are essentially the same. Both forms of prayer require the soul's concentration upon the meaning of the prayer and upon the dedication of the heart during the praying. Granada implies that mental prayer is a higher form of prayer, in part at least, because it is more difficult to maintain concentration when the words are not spoken. He observes, however, that both forms of prayer lose their worth when the mind is distracted. He never implies that prayer has any objective force simply because it is uttered.[5]

At one point near the end, Granada warns his reader that his book is not for everyone. Some of its demands are beyond the capabilities or zeal of some men, and these men should not be condemned by others for not being ready. Nevertheless, most men who intend to lead a life of devotion and who intend to find regular periods to give to prayer are potential targets for his book. One does not need a preliminary course; this book is as basic as one can get.

Instead of trying to lead his reader to the mystical path, Granada seems more concerned with steering people away from thinking of themselves as mystics or potential mystics when they are really ordinary mortals. What should one do if he receives a spiritual consolation while praying? (Fray Luis never defines or describes spiritual consolation.) He asks his reader to consider various possible explanations for the appearance of the consolation. It may be the very natural result of a feeling of tenderness on the part of a sentimental person. It may be the work of the enemy in disguise, trying to confuse. It may be a special gift of God designed to wean the meditator from his worldly ways. It should be considered as a spur, never as a reward. Above all, one should not brag about it. Spiritual consolations should never become a goal. One should be especially cautious about visions, revelations, or rapture. These are probably the work of the enemy. If God wishes to give a person a special message, He will come through clearly. In still another warning Fray Luis states that some men try to cultivate prayer as a kind of art form and even write books upon the subject. He warns against using his own book in this way. For him there is an important difference between a book of guidance and a book of technique. Prayer is too subjective and too personal to be reduced to a formula.

This second part is arranged so that Granada can enumerate aids to achieving true devotion, things which impede it, and temptations occurring along the way. At first glance it resembles a list of platitudes: one should have a great desire for devotion, employ strength and diligence in acquiring it, keep God continually in the memory, etc. It is obvious, however, that Granada is writing from his own experience and thought as well as from the many fountains of his education. He suggests frequent, brief prayers and occasional long ones. He warns against expecting immediate victory over obstacles such as achieving necessary concentration of the mind and will for meditation. He warns both against ignoring and worshipping wisdom. Wherever possible, he teaches by analogy. For example, show a work of fine glass to a man who has never seen anything like it. Tell him a man made it by blowing upon it. Will this man not find the statement incredible? The works of God must be even more wonderful and more incomprehensible. Among the practical suggestions are the following: if you seem to sleep too much, do not try to fight your body; try fasting to see whether this helps you keep vigilant. He is also quick to warn those who seem to be advancing in their path toward devotion, lest spiritual pride and spiritual jealousy enter among the devout. A person is warned to avoid the appearance of piety or any other form of seeming different from his fellow man.

Meditation, therefore, can have a place in the life of anyone. Its efficacy should be measured in terms of the total orientation of man toward God and by its effect upon the various acts and thoughts of the individual. The success of meditation should not be judged by spiritual consolations. (I will define spiritual consolations here as Granada's term for what appears to be evidence of mystical activity or promise.) Granada assumes that of the many who will read his words, more need to be warned against false or premature signs of mysticism than encouraged to exploit mystical signs. Granada must be considered very liberal in one respect, however. Meditation itself is not for him a dangerous practice; instead, it is a natural sequel and companion to regular vocal prayer. The person who has read his warnings against misinterpreting the fruits of meditation or of assigning to it a role of hegemony in the total life picture should be slow to criticize him for writing this book and should applaud him for the fundamental premise that all doors to God should be open to the one who sincerely seeks to serve Him.

IV   *Granada's Study of Prayer: The Exhortations*

The third part of the *Book of Prayer and Meditation* consists of a group of three treatises. The first is on prayer itself, the second, on fasting and self-denial, and the third on alms and mercy. There is something of a recapitulation in these treatises, and it is interesting that Fray Luis continues to stress the relationship between prayer and other forms of expression of a religious orientation. In this way he makes clear that prayer is not a skill that one can acquire or a technique that one can learn. The treatises are an exhortation in which pessimistic assumptions about human nature are minimized, giving a more optimistic ending to the book.

The first treatise is formally divided into the virtue and excellence of prayer, the need for it, and its continuation and perseverance. There seems to be little that is new to us in this treatise except for some unusual, almost poetic, language used in some explanations and exhortations. Several examples involve comparisons between prayer and water. He asks the reader to observe what happens to a sweet basil plant before and after it is irrigated and suggests that the soul may be similarly revived by prayer. He further points out that water is naturally cold and accidentally warm; if it is not kept warm by being close to fire it will soon return to its natural state. Likewise the person who stays close to God through prayer will remain warm in spite of his natural tendency to be cold. Still another example and coming close to St. Theresa's well-known analogy of water and mystic blessings, he points out that the grace of God is more to be compared with rain than with the water that the Egyptians used for irrigation at the time of Moses.[6] Another comparison, showing Granada's growing interest in nature as a manifestation of God's providence is that between the sun and the moon, since the moon has no light of its own but can only reflect the light that it receives. The relationship between God and the soul is similar.

The second treatise, on fasting and corporeal severity, is also divided into three parts: the aids to spiritual blessings, aids to the body itself, and the evils from which man is saved by abstinence. Granada praises self-inflicted punishment as a means of avoiding later penalties which he says will be more severe in Purgatory or infinitely more severe in Hell. He stresses, however, that the most important consideration is not the severity of the punishment but the contrite attitude that the sinner shows to God by means of these self-punishments and self-denials. The second part, directed almost entirely against the harmful effects upon body and mind of overeating, stresses those features of temperance which omit or minimize the religious aspect. Moderation is recommended for longevity, good health, and mental alertness. Granada recalls that Julius Caesar feared the slender Cassius and Brutus for their mental alertness. Granada also points out that true hunger gives a better appetite than can any culinary skill.

The most surprising note, in my opinion, was an observation rather incidental to Granada's lesson on abstinence. He states that in the province of Granada the new Christians live much longer than the old Christians.[7] New Christians for most commentators were viewed with suspicion. They were Christians who had been converted from the Mohammedan or Jewish faiths under pressure of royal decrees. Fray Luis apparently felt that the newly converted tended to live more ascetic lives than their conquerors did and were therefore more sincere in their dedication to a Christian life. In his praise of a life of abstinence and hardship Granada is aware that there is at best a negative virtue in it, stressing, however, that it gives opportunity for the more positive virtues to take hold.

In the final treatise, Fray Luis gives advice concerning almsgiving and mercy. Duty to one's neighbor is not emphasized here. Charity and mercy are a part of one's duty to God and help to assure one's place in Heaven. Granada assures his reader that both for temporal and eternal considerations the one who is generous and merciful will not suffer for it. He tries to steer a moderate path as he gives examples of saints who went to extremities in their charity but suggests that the reader not give more than the receiver needs, that he make reasonable efforts to determine what the needs are without shaming the recipient by excessive prying, and that he perform his act of charity in secret. Fray Luis has other suggestions for guaranteeing the sincerity of the giver. He points out that one who gives merely to discharge the importuner is not being charitable and furthermore is wasting his money. He also observes that he who postpones his generosity until the point of death is not really giving anything. Perhaps most central to his thoughts on mercy is that no man can be judged good by God entirely on the scales of justice. If a man does not show mercy he cannot expect to receive it.

V *Summary of the* Book of Prayer and Meditation

The *Book of Prayer and Meditation* stresses the importance of an integrated life. All approaches to God—prayer, ascetic living, the formalities of the church for public and private devotions, doing good works and acts of mercy—should be given prominence, though some may be emphasized somewhat according to a person's talents, needs, opportunities, or inclination. Granada regards prayer as the integrator of all of the acts of devotion. This book is by no means restricted to those seeking the mystic way. Indeed, some ideas such as the essential identity in function of vocal and mental prayer seem to confound the mystics. Granada's soul is prosaic. He is too concerned with avoiding pride and too conservative by nature to lead his reader up the mystic path until the reader has received a long apprenticeship in ascetic existence.

Such a position made him suspect in the inquisitor's eyes only during the period of the most fanatic searches for heterodoxy and only those who would take passages out of their context could see any threat to the complete orthodoxy in this work. Once a person has thoroughly put into practice all of the ideas expressed here, and if he possesses the temperament of a mystic, he can look to mystical writings with some assurance that his wings are now strong enough for flight.

VI *Granada and Mysticism*

As we approach the subject of mysticism in connection with the works of Fray Luis de Granada, it is well to bear in mind that we are judging him primarily as a writer. We do not want to speculate about his progress up some mystical ladder except in the most general way, because his writings themselves do not invite such judgment or speculation. A mystical experience is extremely personal and comes to our attention only if the mystic tries to capture his experience in literature or in art. The mystic's purpose in doing so is to lead others to a closer relationship to the Power with which he is communing, or perhaps stems from a need to share his joy in the experience. Our interest, however, comes from the ability of the mystic to inspire the nonmystic on a plane analogous with that of the man who may love a woman, nature, music, or anything else, and write about it with inspiration and skill. Mysticism involves an attempt to convey the meaning of an ineffable personal experience. If this experience is not personal, it loses much of its ineffable quality, and consequently for the critic, its literary value. It may retain its interest for the deeply religious man, but for literary or artistic appreciation, its value is considerably lessened.

Fray Luis de Granada is regularly included in any study of Spanish mystics, albeit somewhat apologetically. He does not quite fit the pattern and apparently did not think of himself as a mystic. Often he exhorts his reader to seek fervor in devotion, but always before him is the chasm between earthly and eternal existence. The mystic knows this chasm, but during the mystical experience itself, it does not matter. The mystical experience normally is expressed primarily as an end in itself, rather than an inspiration for improving conduct or for seeking grace.

Why then include Granada among the mystics? Perhaps for the same reason that one studies algebra and geometry before undertaking higher mathematics. Perhaps after studying Granada's writings one can find a new perspective for appreciating an acknowledged giant among mystics such as St. John of the Cross. It may help us to see mystics as human beings, not qualitatively different from those who are not mystics. There is a final reason for studying Granada's mysticism: for the poetry of his thought, a reason that he himself would have disapproved with all the zealousness at his command. Mysticism for the litterateur is the poetry of religion, the link between the religious man and the humanist. Granada warns against excessive interest in humanism. He approves of many aspects of humanism in moderation: the reading of good books, the study of philosophy, finding beauty in nature. Frequently, however, he warns that excess in any good thing is bad, and certainly distilling human pleasure from divine things is wrong in his eyes.

Granada's book, *Memorial de la vida cristiana (Memorial of the Christian Life)*, and its sequel, *Adiciones al memorial de la vida cristiana (Additions to the Memorial of the Christian Life)*, come closest in purpose to that of the mystic way, since their purpose is to show a Christian life which goes beyond what Granada (and presumably the church) requires of all Christians. Granada assumes that every Christian must be fervent enough in his devotion, diligent enough in his religious exercises, and strong enough in his faith to receive the eventual reward of eternal bliss. The person who wishes to go beyond that would be motivated by a love of God rather than rewards and punishments. Some material found in these books is a new presentation of that already found in *Sinner's Guide* or in the *Book of Prayer and Meditation;* much of it, however, deals with acquiring a love that transcends minimal Christianity and any selfish interest.

The Memorial of the Christian Life is divided into seven treatises. The first is an exhortation to live well. It begins with the threats of Hell and the glories of Heaven. This is followed by the blessings in the present life promised to the virtuous. The second treatise deals at length with penitence and confession and the third, with the Holy Communion. The announced purpose is to move toward perfection. Since mysticism is in its way a movement toward perfection, there could be an affinity between mysticism and the progress toward Granada's conception of perfection. If so, he considers the ascetic life a good base for mystics, for surely a mystic is one whose motivation is the love of God.

In the middle treatise Granada analyzes rules for Christian living similar to material already covered in *Sinner's Guide*. His next two treatises are on vocal and mental prayer respectively. The former deals with commentaries upon vocal prayer, followed by a long series of exemplary prayers, a number of which are taken from St. Thomas Aquinas. The treatise on mental prayer uses the life of Christ for the central meditation, a part of which, one will recall, was used for the morning meditations in the *Book of Prayer and Meditation.* Of particular interest in this treatise are his six manners of meditating upon the Holy Passion: "The first the way of compassion, the second of compunction, the third of imitation, the fourth of gratitude, the fifth of love, and the sixth of admiration of wisdom and divine counsel."[8] He suggests that meditating upon the love of God might be more appropriate for the advanced meditators *(los más aprovechados)*. Even here he qualifies his remarks to indicate that all ways may be common to all meditators. Nevertheless, one may consider the seventh treatise as the culmination of the thoughts of the entire book, with the other six being in some degree preliminary material. We will, therefore, look primarily to the seventh treatise for those ideas of Fray Luis which resemble most closely the mystic way.

The mystic progression has been discussed under many frameworks. The one which I have found most understandable is that in which three stages are developed: the purgative way, the illuminative way, and the unitive way. This framework suggests that mystical writers generally agree that the starting point is essentially what Granada has been telling us. One should repent of his sins and try to eliminate from his soul all drives which serve sensual and materialistic purposes. This action makes possible but does not guarantee that a person will move to the illuminative way. The spiritual consolations of which Granada has spoken must be considered glimpses into the illuminative way. This is an indication that the soul feels that God's presence is revealed to him (to her, as many writers express it) in a form that seems more vivid, more personal, or more intense than would ordinarily be experienced. These are usually extrasensory perceptions, though frequently the language of the senses is used to try to describe them.[9]

The unitive way is the way of the small number of mystics who feel that their experiences with God are so personal and so intense that only the analogy of marriage can satisfactorily approximate their recounting. We do not need to dwell here upon this higher form of mysticism since Granada does not seem to have joined this elite company. Those who have reached the highest forms of mystical experience have normally gone through the purgative and illuminative ways and so validated the idea of this progression whether it be called with St. Theresa "the interior castle of the soul," with St. John of the Cross, "the ascent of Mount Carmel," or with others "the mystic ladder."

If the reader accepts the judgment that Fray Luis did not reach the top of this spiritual Mount Carmel, he may wonder, what held Granada back? Aside from the obvious religious answer that it was not God's will, one can with some confidence indicate some qualities in Granada's personality which may have limited him. For all of his great faith he had a scientific mind (which we will consider in detail in a later chapter). Scientific principles of measurement caused him to weigh sins and to suggest that their atonement could also be weighed. He constantly spoke of measure, advocating moderation lest the virtue of achievement be weighed against the sin of pride in the achievement. Granada even worried about mystical consolations lest they be considered a reward for virtue rather than a spur to further virtue.

The mystic *qua* mystic is not conscious of weight, of balancing good and evil. In his love for God he is in no danger of spiritual pride. Perhaps this is precisely because he does not measure degrees of virtue and vice. Furthermore, he is not conscious of serving as a guide for others. While he is conscious of a mystical experience or of a mystical yearning, he is not thinking of telling it, and when he is telling it he is conscious only of trying to describe it, not thinking of it as a lesson for his reader.

Fray Luis never quite forgets his reader, who is his student. For example, in the *Additions*, having said that love is the greatest possible thing, he suddenly thinks of martyrdom. He analyzes martyrdom and concludes that it is a form of love, otherwise it would be a fruitless torment.[10] Another example from the same book speculates that, "If an old lady should find herself at the hour of death with greater love than another who had done many miracles and converted many souls, undoubtedly she would have more essential glory in Heaven since she had had more love on earth."[11]

Some of the comments about Fray Luis which we have used to suggest limitations of mystical attainment could also apply to St. Theresa. She was a person of rare humility and with a genuine concern for her sins. She was also obviously a teacher, and in many of her works was concerned with having the nuns learn lessons from her varied religious experiences. I believe, however, that two differences essential for this analysis emerge between her personality and that of Granada. First, she always has an informal, personal touch in her writing. She was not the scholar that Granada was, and was not capable of the objective analysis that he used. He had many intellectual resources unavailable to her. Second, she was a more emotional individual. Granada's zeal never flagged, but he does not seem to have undergone the intense emotional vicissitudes that plagued or inspired St. Theresa. Therefore, it does not seem whimsical that her mystical experiences were the more striking.

Let us now examine Granada's treatise on love, the seventh and last of the parts of the *Memorial of the Christian Life*—an examination partly for its own sake, and partly in order to evaluate Granada's place in the studies of Spanish mysticism. Love *(caridad)* for Granada is the highest of virtues:

Because our principal purpose in this book has been to form a perfect Christian with all virtues and parts that he is to have, [and] since up to here we have treated all other virtues which are required for this, there remains now for us to treat the main one, which is love, in which consists the perfection of Christian life, with whose perfection one achieves the perfection of this life.[12]

Love of God means taking on the properties of God. Granada cites an unnamed doctor in a strangely baroque-sounding recital of love's many properties,

Love is noble and generous, wise and beautiful, it works great things, it is sweet, strong, productive, simple, chaste, impregnable, and conqueror of all things. Love is all joy, graciousness, delightful, admirable. Love penetrates and breaks, raises and humbles, and conquers all difficulties. Love is high and deep; it wounds and heals; it gives death and life; it cannot be hidden nor can it be paid except with love, and gives all for love because it seeks or wants only love.[13]

Occasionally Granada's exhortations concerning love have a mystical tone, though perhaps it is significant to note that the passages that strike the eye are likely to be quotations such as this one from St. Bernard:

I opened my mouth and attracted the spirit; and sometimes, Lord, while I am closing my eyes, sighing for Thee, you put in the mouth of my heart, a thing that it is better for me not to know what it is. I perceive the taste and the sweetness which comforts me in such a way that if it were given to me in full measure, I would have nothing left to desire.[14]

When Granada uses his own words to speak of the mystical experience, the thoughts become less lyrical, more didactic:

And so the more inflamed the affection of love, and the closer union with God through the experience of love [*por actual amor*] the stronger it resists all other wandering loves which draw it from this love and it will become the more perfect the more it takes on the quality of those sovereign inhabitants of Heaven, who now and forever burn in love with all their strength.[15]

And later, "This love the mystical theologians call unitive because its nature is to join the thing loved in such a way that it finds no rest outside of it, therefore always has its heart placed upon it."[16]

Mystics in general are quick to warn against interpreting psychic phenomena such as visions and voices as signs or messages from God,[17] but Granada is still more cautious since he seems to warn against the real thing.

Very praiseworthy is the fervor of the spirit and diligence is the mother of all good things, but success in any material is dangerous, therefore let man

eat this bread moderately, considering that spiritual food as well as corporeal can have its gluttony. This is said for those to whom this grace is
communicated with full hands, not for those to whom it is given drop by
drop as if distilled.[18]

In the *Additions* Granada does not seek a still higher plane; he
merely elaborates upon his previous themes. Typical of his comments on the nature of mystical love is the following:

Thus the soul which loves God in this manner, comes to be transformed into
God himself in such a way that what He wants she [that is, the soul] wants,
what is displeasing to Him is displeasing to her, what He loves or hates, she
loves or hates. She does not take account of herself for profit, honor, or
contentment, but seeks the contentment of God, His honor, and thus in
everything and for everything comes to have one wanting and one not
wanting, and one will with God; and the will having changed, the life
changes and the works which proceed from it.[19]

Also in the *Additions* Granada expresses the thought that a state of
love, which is similar to mystical love, had been a natural state in
the Garden of Eden. The entrance of sin interfered with this natural
love. Therefore the man who wishes to love God must declare war
against all self-love.[20]

This idea helps make clear that for Granada any love that a mortal
man has for God, even a mystical love, is still a limited experience.
For one to recover the pristine innocence of man before the Fall is
an outstanding accomplishment, but it is put into place and perspective as are all of Granada's thoughts.

Fray Luis, then, has a lofty concept and a practical understanding
of mystical love. Describing it enables him to give his reader, who is
always his student, a presentation of the lofty thoughts of many holy
men and completes, along with theology and asceticism, the picture
of what Granada believes that man needs to know for the salvation of
his soul and for growth in grace.

Fray Luis does not recount his personal experiences in mysticism.
I do not believe that one should draw any precise conclusions about
this reticence. He seemed to understand the mystical sentiments
which he cited from others and could certainly have had experiences
of his own which helped his intuitive understanding of mysticism,
but which he was too modest to express.

In briefly summarizing this chapter, we may conclude that

Granada regards prayer as an extremely important part of a Christian life. He expects the Christian who truly seeks virtue to pray long and often. The prayer may be vocal or mental; it may be original or borrowed. It is not the form in which it is found but the spirit in which it is presented that matters. Prayer should not be considered as a thing apart from other means of seeking a life of virtue such as attendance to religious exercises, works of charity, and devotional readings. In fact, devotional readings, prayer, and meditation seem to blend into each other so that one seems to be a part or phase of the others. Mysticism seems to come out as the expression of man's love for God through prayer. One should be grateful to God for revelations and spiritual consolations, but Granada seems somewhat suspicious of the process of seeking mystical blessings. If prayer helps bring man to a more virtuous life, it has achieved its purpose. All other ambition is superfluous.

CHAPTER 5

Introduction to the Symbol of Faith

GRANADA'S last and longest work is his *Introducción del sím-bolo de la fe* (*Introduction to the Symbol of Faith*). Theologically, this work should be the primary one; a man's behavior should stem from his creed. All of Granada's other works, however, have been based upon an acceptance of the faith. All have been combinations of the theological or philosophical, the didactic, and the meditative. This work, too, will have these qualities, but it will stress the theological and rational, and it almost eliminates that fear, so often expressed in earlier works, that the perverse part of man's nature will hold dominion over him.

The first part of the *Introduction to the Symbol of Faith*, which for many is the most interesting of all Granada's works, shows us his love for nature. He sees no evil in nature. Creatures are antagonistic to each other, but only because each one has an instinct for self-preservation and for the preservation of the species. Nature is complex and shows the mind and providence of God at work, providing for man's needs and pleasure. Granada carefully considers man's place in the hierarchy of God's plan. He is above all other natural creatures since he is made in God's image. He is below the angels, who are pure spirit, but the humanist can almost sense that Granada prefers being a human rather than an angel.[1]

Fray Luis's knowledge of science, whether astronomy, biology, or physics, is based primarily upon what he has read and secondarily upon his own observations. He is not inclined to doubt the knowledge of the ancients in their analysis of the universe and its creatures. One will have to accept with Fray Luis the Ptolomaic astronomy, the four elements (earth, water, air, and fire) the four humors (blood, phelgm, black and yellow bile) and the various interpretations which historically stem from them.[2] The purpose of his exploration of nature is to see God revealed through creation, since

90

our minds cannot really comprehend His infinity. It is tempting to think of this treatise upon nature as a thing apart, but for Granada it has a context—it is part of the basis of faith.

In the second part of this great work, Granada discusses the comparative values of Christianity and other religions. His stress is upon the excellent qualities of Christianity. In his view, other religions are based upon natural speculation and lack the perfections available only in the revealed religion. He ends with the testimony of martyrs and the recording of miracles. The third part tells of the doctrine of redemption from the standpoint of reason and the fourth part, from that of faith. The fifth part is a compendium of the first four.

I   *Understanding Nature as a Way to Understand God*

According to Granada, the highest goal of man is the understanding and contemplation of God. Both the reasoning of ancient philosophers and the lessons of Christianity tell us this. Man's bliss is not found primarily in the absence of vices but in disposing the heart to the reception of celestial things. To study and contemplate the Creation is an excellent way to begin to know the Creator.

Granada likes to show the essential harmony as he sees it between the revealed truth accepted by faith and the reasoned wisdom of the ancients. An appropriate passage from the Psalms reinforces the wisdom of this plan to study nature: "The Heavens declare the glory of God and the firmament shows His handiwork."

Granada suggests an implied question here about faith and reason. If faith is above reason and is the exclusive property of Christians, why should he be so careful to report the reasoning of the philosophers? He observes, however, that there are formal Christians who accept the articles of faith with their intellects but whose works often tend to deny what their intellect confesses. The light of reason should help those whose faith is obscured by evil works.

Basic to Granada's thesis that God's hand is in the creation of the universe—considered entirely from a rational standpoint—is the orderliness of it. This rational approach includes an intellectual antagonist to argue with, in this case Epicurus who, according to Granada, espoused the view that the universe was created by chance. Underlying Granada's view is the assumption that, if the world were created by chance, it would be much more chaotic. As each entity in the universe is considered, Granada will try to show its basic property and function within God's plan and how it serves man in his own life.

In Granada's hierarchy the lowest forms of creation are the four elements: earth, water, air and fire. Next come the mixed imperfects: snow, ice, rain, and winds. Then come the mixed perfects: stones, pearls, and metals. Above these is plant life, which according to Granada lacks feeling and movement. Fifth come the imperfect animals, which have feeling but no movement, such as oysters and other marine creatures. These are followed by the perfect animals, which have movement as well as feeling, such as fish and birds. Seventh in the hierarchy is man, who has reason and understanding. Above men are angels, which also have their respective hierarchy, and God above all.

Before beginning his detailed discussion of the wonders of creation, Granada presents a meditation in which he observes that God is incomprehensible, but that something can be known of Him through the contemplation of His works. Seeking God through nature is a tendency found even among primitive men. Philosophers, in contemplating the beauty and harmony of the universe, are moved to a better understanding of the Creator. Granada does not hesitate to cite philosophers such as Cicero for their accomplishments, in spite of two errors from the Christian viewpoint made by Cicero (and cited by Granada), errors caused by his ignorance of revealed truth: he speaks of gods in the plural and asserts that the gods are not interested in small things. Granada refers to numerous other authorities for their descriptions of nature: Aelian, Aristotle, Pliny, Galen, St. Ambrose, and St. Basil. Ambrose is his indirect source for the comments of Basil who wrote in Greek.

Granada, citing Cicero, asks his reader to contemplate the universe for its beauty and harmony, the vastness of the sea with its wide variety of creatures, and the air, becoming thinner as it rises and in the process forming clouds that water the land. He thinks of the sky with its stars and the principal one, the sun. He considers the special qualities of the moon, which mathematicians calculate as more than half the size of the earth, sending to earth light reflected from the sun and occasionally eclipsing the sun. He then contemplates the fixed stars. All proves that a wise Creator and Governor, not blind chance, brought it into being.

Still following Cicero, Granada speaks of the providential Hand which uses rivers to irrigate the land, citing the Nile, the Euphrates, and the largest of all, the Indus. He sees the hand of God also in other beauties of nature: the tides of the sea, the green of the mountains, medicinal herbs, and other useful products. The harmony of the universe is compared to a chorus of voices, all for man's use—natural evidence that there is only one God.

Fray Luis takes particular interest in the sun. He points out that man is likely to take the sun for granted until it seems to disappear as in an eclipse. A sensitive person, however, can pause to contemplate its beauty and usefulness during its regular appearances. It furnishes light to planets and other stars, and therefore it is God's main creation. It is the indirect cause of rain. It establishes time and seasons, thus arranging for nature's annual growth cycle. The renewal of life each spring is a symbol of eternity. The sun's changes cause spring and fall to be times for the body to adjust between the extremes of summer and winter. The division into day and night also permits man and nature to adjust for continual living.

Granada tells us that the sun is so powerful that even when it is in the other hemisphere it lights the other stars. It penetrates so deeply into the earth that it creates gold, precious stones, and many other things. Therefore, more than any other creation, it exemplifies the providence of God. Granada calls the moon "the sun's vicar," for it controls the tides and regulates the rate of humidity of the trees and of seafood which waxes and wanes with the moon. Occasionally, Granada speaks almost poetically of nature. He recalls that it is much more relaxing in the summer to travel by moonlight even though this light is far less than that of the sun. It is even more beautiful and inducive to contemplating God's care when the moon is absent and one travels with only the light of the stars.

Turning to the four basic elements, Fray Luis puts them into categories in a manner analogous to that of the humors. First, there is the earth which is dry and cold. Next, there is water, cold and humid. Then comes air, which is warm and humid, and finally fire, warm and dry. Each element has strengths and weaknesses, either to work or to resist. For example, a little water can tame fire which otherwise might work too strongly. Earth, with little power to work, has great power to endure. Each has its natural domain. Air, if trapped within the earth, struggles mightily to escape. Air and water, however, mix easily.[3] Each has a natural tendency to mix or to separate, as oil keeps separate from water. Salt mixes readily with water but separates from fire.

Air represents God's providence in providing for the respiratory needs of man and of animals. It is also the medium for the light of the sun or the rain to reach earth. Air is divided into three regions, a very warm region near the region of fire, a temperate region near the earth, and a very cold region between. Winds help with navigation and also carry clouds across vast distances to where rain is needed.

Water provides Granada with innumerable evidences of God's providence. At times, God will make it scarce in order to give man needed lessons in humility. It provides a medium for navigation, with divine providence spacing islands so that sailors may find resting places. For example, St. Helena Island is a very lush place for those en route from Portugal to East India. The sea provides a huge fair and market as countries, separated by water, trade with each other and become interdependent. Many forms of marine life are useful to man, especially for food.

Granada next considers the earth,[4] where men are born, live, and await the final resurrection. Although it is the lowest and least active element, it is the one which serves man most. It produces plants with their fruits, each one with the proper nourishment, protection, and capacity for reproduction. The fields are beautiful as well as useful. The earth provides man with many herbs and stones for medicinal purposes and flowers and some trees merely for man to enjoy their beauty. The fruits and nuts are provided with protection, both for their own sake and for the convenience of man who is to consume them. Trees exist in many forms to provide food for animals, firewood, and shelter for man.

Animals are by definition higher than plants, since they have movement and feeling. Therefore they give even greater evidence of the Creator's work. Operating by instinct, animals often seem superior to man in the performance of actions necessary to self-preservation. Granada gives an example from his own observation of the dog's well-developed maternal instinct. A dog had given birth near his monastery. The monks killed the pups "since there was no need for them" and twice tried to separate the dead young from their mother, but natural instinct caused her to search until she found their bodies and she seemed determined to decide where they should be buried. In the preservation of the species, sometimes fertility rather than strong defense guarantees survival. Others manage to survive either because of weapons for defense or with the use of speed and skill to evade their enemies. Granada cites the example of swallows who appear in Spain in May in such large numbers that one can scarcely imagine how they find enough to eat, but obviously they do.

Fray Luis mentions numerous examples in which the mind of God has planned for animals to survive and to find comfort and convenience. Swans and ducks have webbed feet to get across water easily. Cranes and storks, which have such long legs, have long necks also to allow their beaks to reach the ground. Owls, which search for sustenance at night, have a special light in their eyes. Eagles, flying so high, have exceptional distance vision. Grazing animals know by instinct which plants can be safely eaten and which are harmful. God provides animals with whatever instincts they need: in the case of chickens, it is the rooster's willingness to share food with the hens and the latter with their young. A hen will not share with the young of another brood, while capons grow fat since they feel no need to share at all. Other creatures naturally protect the young or the old. Elderly lions have their children kill their prey for them. Storks use their wings to shade their nests for their young and carry the old who can no longer fly. The pelican feeds its own flesh to its young.

In the case of some creatures, it is trickery which guarantees survival. The crab, searching for oysters, will first hide and then throw a rock at the opening in the oyster so that it can grab the food before closing its shell. The crab, in its turn, is tricked by the fox who sticks his tail into the water to use as bait to attract the crab. Another story of the craftiness of the fox is his method for getting rid of fleas. He will carry a branch into water, gradually wetting his body and encouraging the fleas to take refuge in his facial area. Then, as he also wets his face, the fleas will jump to the floating branch.

Of all animals, the dog is most useful, since he can inspire with his loyalty, be helpful as a hunter, be a friend, and be a simple lap dog for the ladies. One example of the loyalty of a dog which Granada reports is that of a servant who took a dog on a hot August day to an inn to give him water. With every two swallows of water the dog looked around to see if his master was approaching. When he saw his master appear, he stopped drinking and approached him. The lessons to man are: first, man should not willingly depart from his Master; second, when he is forced to leave his Master, his thoughts should be continually upon Him; and finally, he should renounce worldly pleasures when the Master is present.

The elephant is provided with very strong legs which are necessary to support and move his huge frame. Despite his need for his tusks he will surrender them if hard pressed by hunters to save his life just as the beaver will surrender his fur that hunters want. The elephant normally gets his own way, but he has a justifiable fear of the unicorn. The latter sharpens his horn on a rock and, in a fight with an elephant, tries to stab the elephant in the belly. He sometimes fails and the weight of the elephant crushes him, but he succeeds often enough to cause the elephant to flee. Granada speaks of a particular example in Portugal in which an elephant broke an iron grating to find refuge from the unicorn. Thus God gives no animal complete supremacy. The elephant, naturally a modest creature, seeks seclusion for his amorous acts. Any intruder upon his privacy risks his wrath.

Birds likewise show the providence of God in many ways. Some, like the storks, fly in military formation for protection, sometimes with flocks of rooks as friendly escort. Cranes at night leave sentries. Geese, fearful of eagles, spend the entire day with a pebble in the mouth to remind them that they must not make a sound. The hawk on a cold night will hold a small bird captive, simply to take advantage of its warmth. The next morning the hawk, even though hungry, will release the bird and seek food in another direction from the one in which the bird escapes. Perhaps most conclusive of all, the halcyon makes a nest on the seashore. During the week that she sits on the eggs and for one week afterward while she teaches her young to fly, the tides are suspended so that these birds can survive.

Tiny animals show the providence of God more than the larger ones do. Granada wonders that such small creatures can have such differentiated functions which these creatures evidently have, though it is impossible to see more than a speck. Insects are especially useful in teaching lessons to man. The ant makes provision for the winter during the summer months. It builds an underground silo to store things. The seeds that are underground are gnawed so that they will not become fertile while being stored and are carried periodically into the sunlight so that they will not rot in the humid ground. Fray Luis unintentionally made a study of ants in action. He had a jar of preserves in his cell which he tied at the top with very strong paper. The ants found that there was no hole for access, so they gathered an army of diggers to cut holes through the paper to reach the source of the sweet smell. Bees are marvelous creatures, providing valuable honey and wax. They have an organization like that of a monastery with differentiation of labor, regulated hours of activity and of silence, and punishment for those who misbehave or are lazy. They are controlled by a king who receives perfect service. If a king dies, his successor is chosen and rival pretenders are put to death.

Granada asks us to believe in the authority of his sources, Pliny and Aelian, bearing in mind that it is God, not the bees, who is accomplishing these things. Continuing his description of the social organization of the bees, he points out that older bees, who can no longer work, serve as an honor guard to the monarch. The master craftsmen make the honey while less experienced workers seek raw materials. Still others are menials, bringing water for those who work inside the hive. They also have sentinels and guards. During inclement weather the hive is cleaned. On windy days they grab rocks to moor themselves. If they are away from the hive at night, they sleep on their backs so that the dew will not weigh down their wings. If a bee is an offender, a honey thief for example, he is let off with a warning, but persistent wrongdoers are killed. The sick are relieved of normal duties. Bees go out only when flowers are in bloom. They seek good pasture and will dispute possession with a rival swarm. The silkworm serves two functions: to make silk and to preserve the species. The fine silk the worm makes is preserved when it is finished by a substance which prevents it from coming apart when wet. The service of the silkworm is further evidence that God created the animals to serve man.

The examples given in the preceding pages are but a sampling of the numerous ones cited in the *Introduction to the Symbol of Faith*, Part I, but they suffice to show that Granada was well acquainted with ancient books on nature, was very observant of nature himself, and sought a harmony of these readings and observations with what he had learned elsewhere of the nature of God.

Fray Luis next turns to a contemplation and study of the various structures of the human body as a sort of synthesis of all other forms of life and as a culmination of his treatise on the providence of God as revealed in nature. Man is an extremely complicated creature. Granada points out that Epicurus foolishly concluded that our bodies were formed by chance. Ancient sages, whom Granada deemed more reliable, disagreed with Epicurus. These ancient authorities found structural similarities in men, monkeys, and pigs. Modern anatomists (modern for Granada), however, pointed out differences. Fray Luis does not document either the similarities or the differences that he mentions.

Granada makes certain presuppositions for the study of the human body. First, there are three qualitatively different faculties: vegetative, sensitive, and intellectual. Second, ordinary maintenance is necessary to sustain life. Third, communication systems (arteries, veins, and nerves) are essential. Fourth, the body has four humors: blood, phlegm, yellow bile (anger), and black bile (melancholy). Different organs need different amounts of each. A healthy body has a healthy balance of the four. Fifth, the various elements of the body must act in harmony. Sixth, the body has no useless parts.

Granada's study of the human body begins with a description of the symmetry of the sides. The bone structure is such that the two sides are identical. When organs come in twos they are identical, with one for each side. He is impressed by the large number of bones, all formed for their special functions. Fray Luis next goes to a study of the vital organs, beginning with the digestive system. He marvels at its complexity. Different kinds of teeth have their specialized functions to begin the digestive process. The tube which carries food to the stomach is separated from the one which carries air to the lungs. He stresses the importance of the proper flow of yellow bile for the digestive process. He next describes the stomach, divided into ventricles to perform its function. He speaks of the small intestine, surprised at its length and at the number of veins which enter it. He notes with approval that elimination is handled in the most remote area of the body.

Granada discusses the function of the liver, important in the manufacture of blood. The blood is then refined in the heart. Since it becomes very hot there, the lungs send it air to cool it down. The lungs also serve the voice. He compares the larynx to a small bell, and then notices the marvelous qualities of the human voice for speaking and for singing. The lungs also serve for the use of air in the formation of vital spirits sent through the arteries.

Granada considers that there is a qualitative distinction between parts of the body devoted to the vegetative function and those devoted to the emotional and intellectual functions. He sees these as moving from the heavy to the light. The working of the brain is more mysterious than that of other parts of the body. The brain is connected to the spinal cord which in turn is connected to the nerves. The beginning of the brain has an area common to the senses for storing images and other sensory memories. Further on is an area of cognizance, which in animals warns of dangers. This is a sense that goes beyond corporal appearance. Still further back is memory, a special property of man, although some animals enjoy a rudimentary form of it. This area in man is important for science and for prudent judgment. Granada cites examples of prodigious memory such as knowledge of several languages.

Fray Luis then moves to a discussion of the five senses. He is especially attracted by the contemplation of the properties of eyes, which capture such diversified images. In the description of hearing he discusses the eustachian tube, without using this name. He cites Cicero's thoughts on location of the senses, the flexibility of the eyes, the high location of the ears and nose (important since sounds and smells rise), and also the protection which the sense organs have. He then adds his own thoughts about protection such as that afforded by the skin, hair, the covered location of various organs, and speaks of the skill implicit in the human hand. He even mentions the provision made for man to be able to sit down comfortably.

Next, Fray Luis discusses the emotions. Two basic emotions common to all people are love and hate. Hopefully, they serve to help choose the good and reject the bad, giving birth to trust and distrust. They may give us passion to overcome difficulties. There is also fear, to keep the individual from trying to do impossible things or to flee from danger. The person desiring virtue must be armed with the passions (hope, distrust, fear, daring, and anger) to transfer good thoughts into good works. Public justice as well as private feelings are furthered by those individual passions. Man developed honor (a love of virtue) because virtue is not truly virtue if it is motivated by hope of reward. Honor in women centers upon modesty and chastity. Granada points out that some passions have bad names associated with them, but the passions themselves are normally neutral morally. The senses are weapons which the will can use, hopefully with understanding to maintain virtue.

Fray Luis now asks what it means to assert that man is made in the image of God? Man has free will; animals do not. Man has a sense of understanding that other animals lack. He is an artist imitating and adapting nature. He takes advantage of his knowledge of

where things are, how to harness them, and to plan. Man's conversations can overcome time and space. Man is created in the image
and likeness of God. He cannot relinquish the image though he
loses the likeness when he falls from grace. If he does lose this
likeness he is punished for it, often while still on earth. Granada
illustrates this principle by citing the historian, Josephus, who tells
of the unusual earthly punishments of Herod, Nero, and Antiocus,
who, in Granada's view, were given this punishment of severe,
painful illness because of their persecution of Christians. Fray Luis
ends this volume with an analysis of God's perfections and a contemplation of the six days of the Creation. These perfections from
man's point of view are there by definition, since finite man cannot
comprehend the infinite. They are attested to in the Scriptures,
for example in the books of Job and the Psalms.

As Granada contemplates the first day of Creation, he considers
the contrast between the greatest man-made structure, Solomon's
Temple, which took seven years and one hundred and fifty thousand
workers, with the creation of the firmament. On the second day, the
waters receded to where God commanded. The third day was the
day in which plants were created, including those tall straight pines
that serve to build ships that go from Lisbon to the Far East. On the
fourth day, God created the sun, one hundred and sixty-six times
the size of the earth. On the fifth day was created the huge variety
of fish and birds with just a word from God. Man was then created
on the sixth. Granada's thoughts upon creation go from wonder that
the heavens all move around the earth each day to the amazing
potential found in the seed and the egg. He marvels that God placed
the soul within the male only forty days after conception and within
the female after only sixty days. Granada also looks forward to the
day of judgment when God must find all corporeal parts to restore
them for the final resurrection.

It seems reasonable to Fray Luis de Granada to assume that the
wonderful universe, which in his study goes from the sun and the
stars to such tiny creatures as the vinegar worm, came into being
because it was willed in all its intricate detail by the infinite God.
The study and contemplation of the knowledge which the world of
his day held convinced him that every tiny ingredient and entity of
nature was planned by God for order and preservation and to make
life more useful and more pleasant for God's chosen creature—man.

It is likely that few people of his day held a better knowledge of nature than Granada did, since he had read so many works from ancient times, since he had spent so much time observing nature, and since he had such a skill for organization and such keen interest in his subject matter. Sister Mary Bernarda Brentano, commenting upon his attitude toward science says,

In spite of this general tendency to accept theories inherited from the ancients, several statements show a questioning attitude and a belief that observation is necessary in order to learn the causes of what takes place in nature. The author rejects alchemy and is careful to state that future events do not depend upon the stars.[5]

He was an amateur in the study of nature. For Granada, the study of nature was not an end in itself but a vehicle to pursue a better understanding of God.

II *Properties of Faith and Evidence for It*

According to Granada, all men must have a faith to live by. They must believe things they have not seen. There are two manners of obtaining faith—quite clearly he considers one the right way and the other the wrong way. The wrong way he calls acquired, the right way infused. The acquired is the faith of the Moor or the heretic, acquired through many acts of believing what they think or are told and resulting in a confirmation of errors. The other is instilled by the Holy Spirit, and is infused into the understanding of the Christian at baptism. Because of its supernatural origin, it ultimately transcends human reason, but it is possible and profitable to discuss certain excellencies thereof which appeal to reason. Granada lists and describes sixteen excellencies forming the substance of this second part of the *Symbol of Faith*. Of these the ones treated most extensively and which will be our major concern at this point are the witnesses of martyrs, the miracles, and the prophesies.

Philosophy cannot be substituted for religion, says Granada, since philosophers tend to contradict each other. They are to be forgiven for error, since they have only reason to guide them and no orientation outside of mortal life. They should have been able to recognize their limitations of judgment and have prayed for enlightenment. For Fray Luis, the Christian religion recognizes dignity and majesty in its deity. The law (reason) can normally show right from wrong, but it is Christianity, with its Sacraments, which inspires the will to select that which is right. The Christian religion has an ancient beginning and a long history; clearly Granada's Christianity includes the Hebrew background as a part of this history.

There is a chapter on the dignity of the Holy Scripture in which Granada includes a brief synopsis of the Bible, a synopsis which reveals his ability to see it in all its vast perspective. He compares biblical writing with the philosophy of Plato and Aristotle. Despite Granada's admiration for these pillars of Hellenic wisdom, it is obvious that for him they are inferior to the scriptural truth.

The practice of living under the Christian faith is a means of acquiring virtue. Pagans can aspire to virtue, but very few do, and these are imperfect since God is not their goal. Granada admits that unfortunately many nominal Christians do not become virtuous, but the means to virtue are at hand: faith, the Sacraments, prayer, and devotional reading. If one uses these medicines properly, he will get well. Granada finds testimony of the superiority of the Christian life and faith in many places, such as Josephus's *History of the Jews* (admittedly this "evidence" consists of Granada's interpretation of the data, not the author's), from the writings of learned church fathers, and the lives of the martyrs. The biographies of martyrs are a very important part of Granada's symbol of faith. If, as the writer of the Epistle to the Hebrews declares, faith is the evidence of things not seen, a life lived in witness of the faith is evidence that should be very convincing. The recitation of a statement of belief, while one is in a normal church service, may have a certain forthright logic, but the maintenance of similar principles in the face of opposition which seeks by torture to force the repudiation of these principles should have an emotional impact on the reader that far surpasses the strength of reason.

Granada recounts the experiences of a large number of martyrs. There is an often repeated pattern, with names and locations differing. The martyr is called before a judge for failure to render homage to the Roman gods or to Caesar. Especially if the martyr is a young girl, the judge is seized with sympathy for her and tries to persuade her with soft flattering words to abandon Christianity and make sacrifices to the gods. In some cases, male martyrs receive similar treatment. Invariably the martyr refuses, usually in a defiant tone which angers the judge and causes him to order tortures. The one to be tortured is first stripped so that appearing nude in public becomes a part of the punishment, and is then subjected to various kinds of tortures: burning, beatings, and exposure, and for the women, removal of the breasts. These tortures would seem very painful experiences, but the martyr seems to enjoy them because his concentration upon being a witness for Christ is so intense that he seems anesthetized against the pain and other suffering while he has the thrill of knowing that he will receive a great reward in Heaven for such steadfastness. Sometimes the torture is so prolonged that the torturers themselves become weary from their physical efforts and perhaps from seeing the negative results of their work. At times there is divine intervention as the hot irons are cooled or severe wounds are healed overnight. In cases in which the martyr is left to the fury of wild beasts, the beasts themselves seem to know that they are not to harm the martyr. In some cases the judges suspend the torture and try gentle persuasion again, only to return to the tortures when their anger is again kindled by the defiance of the martyr. When the judge finally despairs of breaking the will of the martyr, he orders the martyr beheaded.

A rather special case is that of St. Clement, whose martyrdom is a twenty-eight year saga, traversing a large part of the Roman Empire. Ambition for martyrdom is instilled in Clement by his mother, Sophia. In due course, he is brought before a judge in his native Galatia where the drama already outlined in our composite figure is unfolded. When the judge confesses his inability to break Clement's will, he sends him to Rome where the Emperor Diocletian himself can take charge of the process. A new note enters the recounting of this martyrdom, since the biographer stresses the influence of this process upon the public. The steadfastness of the saint and the utter failure of torturers to break his will have such an effect upon the public that the presence of Clement in Rome becomes an embarrassment to the emperor. He is thus sent to Rhodes where his punishment will attract less publicity. The cycle of cajolings and torture is continued at Rhodes and other places. At one point, under the coemperor Maximian, he is simply left in prison for four years. Torturers tire, judges are frustrated, converts join the saint; at times, authorities fear public uprisings and so the story continues through twenty-eight years, until St. Clement finally dies in his mother's arms.

These stories serve as inspiration for the reader, who has already been given an arsenal of reason to bolster a faith strong enough for a person to dedicate his life to Christian witness. One striking evidence of the importance of the stories of these martyrs is that they are not mere stories to Fray Luis, who contrasts the reading of these true biographies with the reading of the fictitious exploits of those idle books of chivalry with all the lies that they relate. It is not clear to me whether Granada had read any books of chivalry or was merely accepting what he had heard of their reputation. In his own recapitulation of stories of martyrdom, Fray Luis tells us that science exists so that men may know effects by their causes. He sees in these martyrdoms a manifestation of the power of God, since these people with their extraordinary powers of endurance included a cross section of humanity from young girls to very old men. Human strength without divine aid as well as divine inspiration would not have sufficed to overcome these adversaries.

The witness of miracles presents further evidence for faith in Christianity. Granada begins with stories of miracles taken from the Bible. He cites examples such as the cure of Naaman's leprosy, with Elijah as God's agent. He tells of the miracle of Christ's raising Lazarus from the dead and of His feeding of the multitude, but the two miracles that he stresses most from the New Testament are the eclipse at the time of the Crucifixion and the Pentecostal appearance of the Holy Spirit when the apostles spoke in tongues. In the former, Granada stresses the supernatural qualities of the eclipse: its unnatural length—three hours, its unnatural extension—the entire earth, and also the fact, according to Granada's astronomy, that the moon was at that time, on the opposite side of the earth from the sun. Granada sees the symbolic appropriateness of it also; it mourns our loss of the Master and shields his body from public view. In the case of the miracle at Pentecost, it was the ability of each to hear the word preached in his own language that interested Fray Luis. This miracle enabled the message of the apostles to be spread far more quickly. It also showed the courage of men who had not been courageous before.

Granada follows next by recounting many miracles from the various ages since the time of Christ. Imprints of the Cross, the miraculous preservation of a saint's blood, a sweet odor which enabled one to trace a saint's remains, and the miracles wrought by various relics are cited. Some resulted in cures of illnesses, some in conversions to the faith, some in victories over tyrants, oppressors, and infidels. Most accounts are taken from the patristic writings and from the history of the papacy. Granada frequently calls attention to the irrefutable evidence or to the unimpeachable authority of the person telling of the miracle, an implied confession that his reader may need this reassurance of the veracity of the stories.

Some miracles are from Granada's own day. I will cite one to which he attests personally. He tells it in a simple and straightforward manner.[6] At Evora, a convent of Augustinian nuns was very devoted to an image of Jesus as a child. One of the nuns, still alive as Granada writes, became very ill and later crippled. All medicine proved futile and all doctors helpless to effect a cure. One Christmas she began to feel that Jesus planned to cure her. In the presence of the image, she suddenly found that she could walk without the aid of her crutches. Granada further writes of a Portuguese woman who was possessed of a demon. A bishop, working hard to exorcize the demon, learned that this woman had not been baptized because of some disorder at the time that the baptism had been scheduled. After the baptismal ceremony had been performed, the demon departed.

For Granada the culmination of the history of miracles is the conversion of the world. Could the world be convinced that the son of a carpenter, one who died on a cross between two thieves, was God? Could twelve fishermen, not especially endowed with leadership, wisdom, or courage make the world believe? Could believers overcome the opposition of all idols and their worshippers and of emperors determined to eradicate Christianity? Since the answers were all affirmative, it can only be that the power of the Holy Spirit was at work in the world for this miracle to be achieved.

After the witness of the miracles comes the witness of prophesy. Prophesy ultimately comes from God, since only He has the ability to determine the future which he has retained in spite of his gift of free will to mankind. Apparently Granada sees no inconsistency in the belief in the omniscience of God and the free will of men. He believes that the fulfillment of prophesy is the strongest evidence for faith, since a person of his day can see the results of this fulfillment as well as turn back to the time in history when the prophesy was proclaimed. Among these prophesies are the veneration predestined for Mary Magdaline and for Mary, the Mother of Christ. Others are the prophesies concerning the establishment of the church and the destruction of Jerusalem. In Granada's conclusion to this second part, he speaks of the harmony of faith comparable to that of music. Perhaps Granada's most important idea concerning the religious life is that of harmony among its various elements. Faith, reason, works, charity—all are good things, all in their proper measure.

III *Fruits of the Cross*

The first and principal treatise of the third part of the *Introduction to the Symbol of Faith* deals with fruits of the tree of the Cross. Granada makes varied, interrelated uses of it. The first of these is theological: God created man as the only creature capable of understanding what divinity is. He was not created with the imperfections of original sin but with freedom of will, therefore with the ability to sin. Since God knew from the beginning that man would fall from grace and need a Redeemer, He planned in the beginning for this Redeemer. Christ's incarnation, life, and crucifixion constituted from the beginning God's plan for man's redemption. Granada maintained that it was not the only way that the Redemption could have been accomplished, but it was the way God chose, and it has noticeable advantages for helping man to see what his relationship to God is, for helping him to take advantage of the example that Christ showed through His earthly life, and to serve as inspiration to man as he tries to live a virtuous life. Since the Cross was in God's plan from the beginning, the story of the Bible and of the church can be studied with the Cross in mind. Thus, allegorical interpretations can be made of Old Testament stories to show how they point toward the time of the Cross. Perhaps most central to this treatise is the fact that, by placing this story of the Cross into various settings, one can see fruits of the Cross in spiritual lessons and inspiration.

Granada points out that reason (that is, theology) harmonizes well with faith in the story of original sin and man's consequent need for a Redeemer. He sees man as having been created without imperfections and given reason, a quality other creatures lack. It was natural for man to choose things proper to his own pleasure and profit, but since he was composed of body and soul, the things good for the soul often differed from those in which the body took delight. The spirit should prevail over the body; man's purpose should be to contemplate God and, in doing so, to accept the moral virtues which control the passions. Therefore, seeking to contemplate God and to live virtuously is to live an integrated life.

Granada tells us that philosophers have wondered how God could have made man so imperfect, but Christianity tells us that God has not done so. We were born with these passions and with some tendency to let them get out of control as a result of original sin. Not only men but also some angels rebelled against God. God did not try to save Satan since Satan by his nature was incorrigible, and he sinned without having a temptation from an outside source, but man is capable of change, while diabolic sin is induced by an outside temptor. Having decided to redeem man from his sin, God (as Granada interprets it) decided that for the sake of justice, only He himself could be the redeemer and the atonement. Neither man nor angel could provide the redemption. By having God become man, divine and human justice are combined. Furthermore, if man's pride caused his fall, it is fitting that God's humility should redeem it.

Granada reasons that God, having redeemed man, did not want the benefits reserved to the Jews, and gave his apostles the command to evangelize the world, sending the Holy Spirit to help them. Man, receiving the gift of redemption purchased by God himself, acquires dignity from the redemption and a responsibility not to misuse it.

A large part of the first treatise of Part III is the presentation of the tree of the Cross. The various fruits of the tree, twenty in number, represent a rather strange mixture of units. Some are theological qualities such as man's having a divine high priest and advocate, having the Sacraments, or enjoying revealed knowledge—unavailable through philosophy. Others are general qualities such as hope, patience, or humility, which might not need the Cross for their validity, but which Granada feels are exemplified in a special way through the Cross. Still others are symbols of the nature or way of the Cross: the profession of austerity or the Cross as a subject for meditation. Finally, these fruits include general and specific aids, such as help against temptation, or examples for the Christian to follow, both the example of Christ and those of the Christian martyrs.

Thus, for Granada, the story of the Cross is the staging of a drama planned from the beginning. Its primary purpose was man's redemption, but there were important secondary purposes, because this drama serves for man's instruction and inspiration. Finally, woven in there is a kind of theory of history. Christ's life was God's invasion of history. In addition to this invasion, there is the Old Testament account of Christ's predecessors, many of whom commit-

ted acts which can be fully understood only as symbols or lessons for
Christians to understand much later than the acts as such and
perhaps not known to the performers themselves.

The second treatise of this third part furthers this theory of history
by dwelling upon the activities of specific men and women of the
Old Testament which, in Granada's interpretation, teach lessons
about the coming of Christ. In earlier works, Granada had occasionally referred to Christ as the true Samson, when speaking of
strength, or to the true Solomon, when referring to wisdom. Here,
for Granada, the story of Eve shows us that just as she was created
from Adam's side, the church is created from the side of Christ. The
death of Abel shows symbolically the death of Christ, since the Jews
who killed him were "his brothers." Noah saved mankind through
his Ark; Christ later saved mankind through the Cross. Jonah was
also a Christ figure, his three days in the "whale" representing the
duration of Christ's death. Other examples abound. All show that
characters and events of the Old Testament appeared and occurred
to enable Christians to see that this history is an important part of
the story of God's concern for man.

The final treatise in Part III is a dialogue between a teacher and a
pupil. The rapport between the two is excellent; the pupil invariably
expresses thanks and gratitude for the answers to his questions
while the teacher seems gratified by the student's ability to understand. Granada's purpose, however, seems not drama, but simply
review. Answers predetermine the questions. One basic point is
uppermost in Granada's mind in this treatise: he imagines that
someone outside the Christian faith might consider that the hum-
bling process of the redemption (God becoming man, living humbly, dying on the Cross) somehow takes away the dignity that becomes the Deity. Granada's answer is a thorough refutation of this
proposition. Man gains dignity by such association but God never
loses any.

One of the pupil's questions, for example, is why God did not
send a lesser messenger than his Son. The answer is that God did
send the prophets along with warnings, punishment, exile, but
throughout, the Prince of Darkness seemed to prevail. God felt that
unless He sent Christ, He would lose the battle for man.

A corollary question concerns why God assumed human form,
especially that of a newborn child. Granada's answer, here as
elsewhere, is that of separating the physical and spiritual aspects of

man. The things which seem important to man—pomp, physical power, wealth—are as nothing with God. Furthermore, the use of the humble to overcome the proud is in itself dramatic and will make an impression upon those whom Christ is trying to reach.

In these discussions Granada tells us that Christ's passion was painful to him *qua* man but not *qua* God. The humbleness of Christ's life and death confounds the Jews since their concept of a Messiah is one who is rich and powerful. Thus Christ controls man's excessive love of honor (pride), property (greed), and pleasure (lust). The basic theme of Part III is accordingly to advise acceptance of the church's explanation of man's fall and his redemption through the Cross. It is truth revealed by God; it is equally worthy of credit in that it has been presented to man in a reasonable, rational way.

IV *Faith and Prophesy*

Granada always stresses the importance of balance between reason and faith. In the third part, he considers that he has stressed reason; he declares that he is here stressing faith. He seems to try to make reasonable interpretations, but the witness of prophesy tells him that God has told the prophets what to say so that man can later say that what they predicted came true. The fulfillment of prophesy is one of the important links in the chain of Granada's exposition of his faith.

It seems to me that Granada overlooks one important element in prophesy: preventive prophesy. Certainly this element lies outside his present purpose. By "preventive prophesy" I mean that a prophet will forecast doom in the hope that people will repent and thus avoid the consequences feared and predicted. For example, we have the amusing witness of Jonah's predicting dire things for Ninevah. To his surprise they repent and God withholds punishment. Jonah is upset that his predictions did not come true (see Jonah 4:1). Granada's interest in prophesy is to show that God has given man cause through prophesy to believe in His omnipotence and that He will surely punish those who turn from Him.

The prophesies in Granada's account serve to stress the relationship between the two Testaments. The entire fourth part is concerned mainly with convincing convertible Jews that the proper interpretation of their common legacy will permit them to understand and believe Christianity. These prophesies are divided into many categories. First is the Incarnation. The most graphic prophesy comes from the Book of Isaiah, praised by Granada for its elegant style, but other Old Testament references abound. Facts about the life of Christ and predictions of His death are also foretold. Perhaps most significant of all are the prophesies of the spread of Christianity as a result of Christ's life and death.

The first of these results was the discrediting of both the Roman deities and the worship of the Emperor. Granada discusses the life-style of these gods, especially of Jupiter, who used various disguises to trap unsuspecting maidens. Fray Luis suggests that if the various examples of deceit practiced by these deities were emulated by their subjects, the inevitable result would be rampant immorality. A second result was the worldwide publicity given the true God, the God of the Jews. Granada notes that Christianity became truly the universal religion when it was recognized by the Roman Empire under Constantine. All of this represents the fulfillment of prophesy. A third result of Christ's coming was the new morality. Granada gives a detailed account of the righteous lives of monks, especially those in the Egyptian desert in the early centuries. He admits that not all achieved the virtue of these monks, but he suggests that the contrast between this life and the old immorality was startling.

Granada's most intensive and extensive treatment of prophesy and its fulfillment concerns the punishment of the Jews. The Old Testament is full of examples of God's warning to the Jews not to turn from Him. They should have known to expect punishment. Above all, they were expecting the Messiah as their Scriptures show. Granada tells them that the Messiah was to appear at the end of the dynasty of Judah. The appearance of Herod indicated that the dynasty of Judah was at an end. The Jews did not recognize the Messiah when He came but put Him to death. Granada utilizes Josephus's history to tell the gory tale of God's vengeance upon them for this death. As Granada points out, Josephus is also a non-Christian witness for the historicity of Jesus. Josephus apparently did not meet Jesus but heard of Him and reported the existence of His band of followers. Granada also mentions the belief that Virgil predicted the coming of Christ.

The punishment which the Jews suffered, following Granada's interpretation of Josephus's account, was caused, in the immediate sense, first by internal dissension and strife and second by a fanatical attitude toward the Romans. Granada pictures these Roman rulers as strong and determined soldiers who wished to conquer and rule but not to be consciously oppressive. The fanatical efforts of the Jews to preserve their independence seemed not noble but treacherous. They suffered death in battle and death from starvation. Clearly their killing of Christ was the crime which God was avenging. In the fifteen hundred years since that time they have suffered exile and now (Granada's time) they are generally despised.

Fray Luis does not believe that an individual Christian should add to their persecution: "However, in this place Christian charity and the zeal for salvation of souls obliges me to warn those who, jealous for the Faith, believe that they do not sin by doing harm to those outside the Faith, be they Moors, Jews, Heretics, or Gentiles. They [the infidel] are neighbors [*prójimos*] just as the faithful are."[7] Later, Granada gives an example of the reasoning of a Jew converted in his time. This man says that the Jews were accused of the death of the Savior. The Jews have been severely punished. If they had not been guilty, God would not have allowed this punishment. Therefore this man accepts the Christian faith.[8]

Fray Luis notes that if suffering were evidence of guilt, he has a problem in explaining the suffering of the martyrs, but he points out that these people did not really suffer since their spirits never flagged and their promise of reward was great. The final evidence of faith from prophesy is the prediction of Christ's coming made by the Roman sibyls. Granada feels that if someone thinks that Christian zealots made up all of these stories, the skeptic has but to consider the confirming evidence of these disinterested sibyls (all virgins) as well as the testimony of Josephus to know that all these biblical prophesies and histories are true.

The second treatise in Part IV is a dialogue between the teacher and a catechumen, a converted Jew who is trying to improve his understanding of the Christian faith. The neophyte is thrilled and grateful for the explanations. Sometimes he seems to ask questions which deal with things that puzzle him; at other times he asks for answers to objections placed by Gentiles. This treatise is more than a catechism, because the answers contain reasoning and a psychological approach. Since the catechumen is thoroughly converted and disciplined, the teacher has no worries about insulting the Jewish race or beliefs. Granada does try to show some respect for the Jews, however, especially the pre-Messianic ones. Fray Luis recalls that Jacob (Genesis 32) had one game leg as a result of his struggle with the angel. He explains this as prophetic, foretelling first, the split between Israel and Judah, and second (after Christ's coming), the split between those who accepted Him and those who did not.

In the course of this explanation of the superiorities of Christianity vis-à-vis Judaism, Granada has sharp criticism for the Jewish *Talmud*, pointing out features which seem alien, not only to Christian theology but to theological dignity and to common sense. Granada's knowledge of the *Talmud*, apparently, is secondhand. His source is a commentary, not a translation. Imbued as he is with the strong sense of the link between the people whom he considers guilty of Christ's death and those who wrote the *Talmud* he cannot be expected to give a useful interpretation of its teachings. It is almost his view that the only good Jews since the time of Christ were Christian Jews. One exception which he notes is that of a Jewish doctor who had been treating St. Basil. This doctor, from Granada's viewpoint, was a wonderful man whose only flaw was his stubborn insistence upon remaining faithful to the religion of his parents and family tradition. This doctor had done all that he could for St. Basil, but it was now time for St. Basil to die. The doctor told him that he would die before sunset. St. Basil had, of course, been trying to convert him to Christianity. He asked if there were any chance that he could live another day. The doctor assured him that it was impossible; it would be a miracle. St. Basil asked God for this miracle. He was still alive the next day. St. Basil accepted the doctor's conversion, baptized him, and gave him communion. It was then possible for St. Basil to die in peace.[9]

Another issue treated intensively concerns explanation of the Trinity. On other occasions, Granada has mentioned that this mystery was a difficult one to understand. One should pray to God for permission to think about the Trinity as entrance into a sanctuary. It is one of the things to be taken on faith without a complete understanding by reason. Granada gives the biblical references to the Trinity. He avoids a precise interpretation but gives some guidelines. When we hear of the Three Persons we should not think in corporeal terms. The concept of God is so vast that it is difficult for man's mind to grasp it. This explanation, as well as others on the relationship of faith and reason, show Granada as a good Thomist (as we would expect of a Dominican friar).

Since the major difference between Judaism and Christianity is Christ's incarnation, Granada dwells at length upon Christ's earthly life. He feels that there were enough Old Testament prophesies to indicate clearly that the Messiah was to come at the time of Jesus's birth. He assumes that the humility of Christ's birth, life, and death could be a stumbling block for a Jew trying to accept Christianity. He explains that by insisting upon this humility, God is reminding us that the pomp that impresses man is not a part of His plan, but that the lesson in humility is proper for man's guidance.

Another area of concern for Granada is the transition from Jewish law to Christian theology. It is surprising that he does not stress St. Paul's teaching on the subject (Romans 7). Has the Jewish law been repealed? If so, does that mean that God has changed his mind? Granada says that the law is divisible into three areas. First, there is the moral law, which is unchangeable. Second, there are the laws about customs which are subject to change, especially when the area under their jurisdiction is enlarged to include people with differing backgrounds and needs. The third area, also changeable, is the judicial process in which punishments are decreed. Granada further explains that a people as well as an individual can have stages of life. God chose the Israelites when they were young as a nation; they needed a different kind of guidance when they became more mature.

Still another feature of Christianity dealt with the Sacrament of bread and wine. Granada says that there is no explanation in human terms of the process by which the bread and wine become the body and blood of Christ. He does say that the reverence for the sacrament is less for the sacrament itself than for the presence of God that is recognized in the sacrament. The catechumen asks whether the Jewish law was as good for the ancient Jews as Christianity is now for us—thus setting up the climax for this treatise. The teacher, apparently a student of Plato, answers that there is no comparison; they had the shadows; we have the light of truth.

V *Granada's Recapitulation*

In four large volumes, Granada has covered the subject of Christian faith. He decided to summarize each book in a treatise. Presumably this compendium serves the dual purpose of providing a short form for those who lack the time or patience to read the four volumes as well as a review for those who have read the first four. The first of these treatises is a true compendium of the first volume. The treatise is about one-seventh the size of the original volume and summarizes the material faithfully. This is the study of creation intended to serve as a vehicle for the better understanding of the nature of the Creator.

The second treatise begins with the same plan. Granada tells in briefer form the excellent qualities of the Christian religion, just as described in the second volume. A large part of the second volume, however, is devoted to further stories of martyrs. Upon approaching this material, Granada veers from his purpose, since there are so many other martyrs whose stories have inspired him. His compendium is faithful to the lessons of the second volume, but this part of it is almost as long as the part he is summarizing, while all of the examples he uses are new. There is one innovation in that one of the martyr stories portrays a virgin brought before a judge so overcome by the steadfastness of the virgin that he is converted and joins her in martyrdom.

Of special interest to us in this area is a new locale for martyr stories: Elizabethan England. Here the martyrs face persecution by the Queen's agent, a viscount. The martyrs are described as patient and loyal to their country in every respect except where such loyalty seems to conflict with a higher loyalty—to their church. One of these martyrs is quoted as saying that Christ did not use English when he prayed.[10] When Granada refers to the anti-Catholics in England, he normally refers to them as heretics. On one occasion he refers to them as Calvinists.[11] He does not go into detail here or at any other point to enlighten his reader on the subject of heresy. There seems to be only heretics, not varieties of heretics. In this fifth part he does give a clue to the cause of heresy, saying that man is a rational creature and resists the idea of believing those things which his rational powers cannot grasp.[12]

The third treatise attempts to summarize the material in the third volume of the *Introduction to the Symbol of Faith*. The third volume was organized around an allegorical idea: that the Cross of Calvary is a tree with varied forms of fruit which are valuable to man. It also attempted to give an explanation appealing to reason explaining the process of man's creation, fall, and redemption in such a way as to deny either that God was in any way responsible for original sin or that redemption was a correction of a divine error anticipated and planned for by God. The description of the redemption is a theological lesson which, in addition to its primary purpose of redeeming, gives valuable examples to guide man's conduct. The recapitulation attempts to explain Granada's views again but does not use the allegory of the

Cross in the process. This treatise, like the one preceding, is rather long to qualify as a compendium.

The final treatise, like the first one, is a true compendium of the corresponding volume which he summarized. In this case it is the faith which is based upon the fulfillment of prophesy and is especially directed to Jews in the hope that they will see Christianity as the fulfillment of the prophesy of their own prophets.

Occasionally an expression or a summarizing thought in this fifth volume captures the fancy. Granada thinks of Christianity in its beginnings as presenting its appeal to Jews and Gentiles alike. In his words, the idolatry of the Gentiles offends the Jews while the rigidity of Jewish law offends the Gentiles. Christianity removes these two objections, subsuming them in love (*caridad*) to unite these divergent and irreconcilable groups.[13] In his discussion of the power of love, Granada surprises with a comparison with secular love, quoting Ovid to show how Dido's soul was inflamed with love for Aeneas. Divine love, of course, should be stronger.[14]

Granada surprises us further by a comparsion between the severity of the torture suffered by Christian martyrs with that suffered by backsliding Jews during the time of the Catholic sovereigns. The Inquisition, according to Granada, proceeded with mercy and justice in its efforts to keep religion pure. Those who had to be put to death were burned quickly, not given a prolonged torture.[15] If this note had been by Cervantes, one might have detected subtle irony, but with Fray Luis one must assume that he truly felt that the Holy Office combined justice and mercy in its operations. Perhaps the significant note here is that Granada felt defensive enough to include this contrast.

The position of Satan is a difficult one for any Christian theologian to analyze. Granada calls him the Prince of the World. He was an angel who rebelled and while he has always had power, it is controlled and derivative. Granada makes clear that God, not the Devil, is in charge, even in Hell. He calls the Devil God's jailor.[16] A good final summary of the book of faith comes in these words: "God has created two worlds, one natural, which is this which we see filled with so many things, and another supernatural, which is the Catholic church, adorned with its sacraments, with the Holy Scriptures, the examples of Christ and of His saints, and with the presence of the Holy Spirit.[17]

CHAPTER 6

Miscellaneous Writings

I *Granada as a Biographer*

A somewhat new picture of Fray Luis de Granada is revealed through an examination of his biographies. The biography of Fray Bartolomé de los Mártires is relatively short. One can feel sure that his purpose is almost entirely to preserve the memory and deeds of his friend and to present a living example of what for Fray Luis seemed a model Christian life. An unintended side result is a rather sharp criticism of the conduct of men in high places, both among the nobility and the upper echelons of the church.

Granada does not give us the date of Fray Bartolomé's birth. In 1527, he entered the convent and made his profession two years later. Apparently he was born in 1514, since he professed at the age of fifteen. His advancement was in education and administration, since he became a master of theology and prior of his convent. Granada reports that it was a concern of the queen (Catalina) to obtain for the archdiocese of Braga a prelate of pious life and charitable ways; in this way she hoped to avoid an appointment based on political influence and ambition. Fray Luis does not report that the queen asked him to take the position of bishop of Braga, as related by his biographers, but he does tell us slyly that the man who was confessor to the queen (himself) persuaded Fray Bartolomé to accept the bishopric.

As archbishop of Braga Fray Bartolomé was forceful and forthright in denouncing public scandal even when the misconduct was performed by influential people. Fray Luis hints that Fray Bartolomé was caught in a political bind because, on the one hand, he had been tutor to Don Antonio, a pretender to the Portuguese throne, and on the other hand, he felt a sense of loyalty to Philip II, who had seized the throne. Siding with the Spaniard naturally made him unpopular with many Portuguese. Granada cites this problem as evidence that personal considerations were cast aside when Fray Bartolomé faced difficult choices.

The bishop visited remote places which his predecessors had considered inaccessible. He was thus able to help people who had been neglected. He lived frugally and was very generous with the poor. He furthered monastic life and advanced theological education. The highlight of Fray Bartolomé's life was a trip to Trent to attend the important council of the church which was held there. Granada does not use Fray Bartolomé's participation as an excuse to comment upon the far-reaching decisions of the council but merely to tell of Fray Bartolomé's role there and at Rome. The archbishop was disturbed by those in high church positions who lived lives of great luxury and even dared suggest that the pope himself could show an example of greater frugality. The words which Granada used to describe this criticism of the pope are a model of diplomacy, though Erasmus himself could hardly have expressed it more forthrightly:

Self-love is so ingenious that it always finds good reasons and a color of piety for the things that it wants; and it is so subtle that, as the saints say, it gets into everything, even into very divine exercises, without its being realized; consequently, those who enter most carefully into the service of God and wish to offer Him a pure and clean sacrifice live always very wary of this adversary that they carry within them and examine very carefully the intent that they have in order not to deceive themselves with the appearance of good.[1]

When he became old, the archbishop asked Granada to intercede for him in order to be able to retire from his duties. Permission was granted and he lived his remaining years in simplicity and peace of mind. The last chapter in the biography had to be written by another hand, since Granada died two years before Fray Bartolomé did. In general Fray Bartolomé exemplified a life-style and conduct that Fray Luis both admired and practiced. Fray Luis admired but apparently did not emulate the archbishop's habit of administering stinging reproof to the influential who led lives which were not examples for others to follow.

Juan de Avila, one of Granada's earlier heroes, was the only child of rather wealthy parents, but from a very early age showed signs of desiring an ascetic life. He was sent to Salamanca to study law but soon showed a preference for the church. He was persuaded to go to Alcalá to study the arts. Upon the death of his parents he gave his entire inheritance to charity and decided to become a preacher, taking St. Paul as his model and guide. Although Juan de Avila lived the austere life of a monk, there is no mention by Granada of his joining a religious order.

As Avila's biographer, Granada seemed almost exclusively interested in the discussion of his personal qualities which made him an influential preacher rather than in the recording of the events in his life. Granada speaks of Avila's love of God and of his fellowman and of the evidence of his holy life and effective preaching, which can be found in Avila's letters. Granada does give some details of Avila's preaching in several cities: Granada, Baeza, Córdoba, and Montilla. Fray Luis also describes briefly the lives of several important citizens who were influenced by Juan de Avila to devote their lives to Christ or who were sustained in the practice of this life.

Perhaps the most significant detail mentioned in the biography is his reference to St. Theresa. Fray Luis mentions her as a great servant of God, persecuted at first by those who did not understand her spirit. He then briefly mentions the aid that Juan de Avila gave her in this time of trial, comforting her and reassuring others of the rightness of her cause.[2] Granada stresses Juan de Avila's interest in furthering religious education and in the inspiration which he provided for young people who aspired to an austere life. Avila is pictured as a friend of all mankind but most particularly of those who had fallen into sin and needed his help to turn back to Christ.

Virtually the only event in Avila's life which Granada reports in detail is his death. He describes the hourly increase in the suffering and Avila's forebearance and humility as he approached death. His death occurred in May, 1569, some years after Granada had left Spain for Portugal. Presumably he had had assistance in following the details which he reported.

The sixth treatise of the *Memorial of the Christian Life* is a study of mental prayer with the life of Christ as material for meditation. Later in the *Additions* the life of Christ is used in a longer meditation. Fray Luis presumably did not think of these as biographies in the sense that the books on the lives of Juan de Avila and Bartolomé de los Mártires were. The main difference was that Granada's works were the only readily available sources for the lives of the two Iberians while the story of Christ's life was available elsewhere. Granada's recapitulation of the events in Jesus's life could be used as a regular biography, however, starting with the prophesies of His coming and following with a fairly chronological account of the re-corded events of His life.

Granada does not speculate about those years not represented in the records. In the period of Christ's ministry between His baptism and the passion of Holy Week the biography (in both places) is highlighted by Christ's relationship with four women: a Canaanite, a Samaritan, the woman taken in adultery, and Mary Magdalene. All seemed to be helped through faith. They were representative of the deeds and spirit of Christ's ministry, since they were either not of the chosen people or else they had sinned and thus forfeited this status. Therefore, they were the kinds of people that Christ would have ministered to when other religious leaders would have re-jected them.

Biography, then, forms a minor part of Granada's writings. The events of a man's life are always to be subordinated to the religious lessons that they may teach or to the value of meditating upon the love that inspired them. They serve us in showing that Granada admired certain actions in other people that modesty would not have allowed him to imitate. Otherwise, they reinforce the lessons that he teaches elsewhere.

II *Granada as Translator*

Fray Luis began his writing career as a translator in 1538, many years before he started publishing original works. His first transla-tion was called either *Contemptus mundi* or *De Imitatione Christi* attributed to Thomas à Kempis. Though *Contempt for the World* is the more descriptive title, the work is now known as *The Imitation of Christ*, probably because the first sentence of the text advises the reader to imitate Christ's life and customs.

Meditating upon *The Imitation of Christ* is the mental equivalent of wearing a hair shirt; its succinct, pithy messages are barbs that prick the heart of the conscientious. It was written from the point of view of a devout monk who held the world more in fear than in contempt. It has the candor of the moral pessimist combined with the love of God that longed to be mystical but could never break free from the consciousness of worldliness and from the spiritual modesty of one who fears temptation even when he does not feel tempted. It is easy to see why Granada was inspired by this work. Granada admired Kempis just as he admired Bartolomé de los Már-tires and Juan de Avila, for that austerity which challenged, perhaps even whetted his appetite for, his life of self-denial. There is a harshness or perhaps starkness which Granada never quite achieved in his own writing that comes through in almost every sentence of *The Imitation of Christ*. The impact of the work is greatly increased by its utter sincerity. Kempis is severe in dealing with everyone, himself most of all. Granada's soul was oriented in the same direction, certainly concerning his demands upon himself.

By this translation, Granada displays the two most necessary assets: a thorough knowledge of Latin and a mastery of the rhetorical handling of Spanish. Apparently there were few problems of manuscript variants. One can easily compare his translation with a Latin text available today.[3]

There is, however, a temperamental difference between Kempis and Granada as revealed in their writings. Kempis worked slowly, methodically, carefully polishing each sentence to make it a complete unit for memorization and meditation—the product of an age which did not know the printing press. Granada, with his Ciceronian language, and with the power of the new press, must have felt that his wings were clipped with the terse style of the *Imitation*. The Latin suggests the poetic parallelism of the Psalms. Granada usually recaptures this rhythm: *Gran cosa es el amor, gran bien para toda cosa* ("A great thing is love, a great good for everything"). Occasionally, however, the parallelism is lost where Kempis writes, *Praeter amare Deum, et illi soli servire* ("Except to love God and to serve only Him"), Granada translates, *Si no amar y servir a solo Dios* ("Except to love and serve only God"). Such lapses in the catching of the rhythm are few.

Even rarer are the occasions in which Granada mistranslates. On one such occasion, I suspect that he felt that he was making a correction: Kempis has *Amans Deum anima, sub Deo despicit universa* ("The Soul loving God, despises all things beneath Him"), which Granada translates *El ánima que ama a Dios, desprecia todas las cosas sin El* ("The soul that loves God despises all things without Him"). Granada thus slyly removes what would have to be considered an exaggeration, by changing the preposition. Granada's translation has been in part superseded by that of the Jesuit father Nieremberg, composed a century later. Many later editions, however, yet attest to the continuing popularity of Granada's version; the one with the widest current circulation is probably the *Aguilar* edition, in the *Colección crisol*, modernized by the Dominican friar, Luis G. Getino.[4]

The Imitation of Christ is still widely read today. Granada's other translation *Escala espiritual (Spiritual Ladder)* has not developed comparable appeal, although Granada's translation is considered a superior work to his translation of the *Imitation*. At the time of this translation Granada was a far more experienced writer than when he wrote the *Imitation*. His stated reason for translating this work, given in his dedication to Queen Catalina of Portugal, was his dissatisfaction with existing translations, one archaic and the other full of errors. Granada's first idea was to correct the existing Castilian version, but he discovered that he needed to compose a new translation with frequent references to the original. It would be interesting to discover what he meant by the word "original." He pointed out that the work was originally written in Greek and that, of two Latin translations, the one by Camaldulense was preferred as more modern. Was Granada versed in Greek or does he merely refer to the Latin translation here? Since none of his biographers refers to his knowledge of Greek it would be presumptuous to credit him with fluency in Greek. He refers to John Climacus's name as being Greek for ladder. Later we will show other references to his interest in Greek words. He apparently had some acquaintance with the Greek language but did not feel qualified as a Greek scholar or translator.

Granada's confidence as a translator goes beyond criticizing his predecessors as translators. He refers to the intrinsic difficulties of translating this work, and on several occasions he has placed at the end of a chapter a summary or interpretation of the chapter he has just finished. In one of these chapters (the fourth) Granada expressed a warning to the reader against literal application of its advice. He noted that times change and that his time demanded a somewhat more relaxed approach. Since the *Spiritual Ladder* was written for a monastery, Granada was especially careful to warn those ladies not professed against fanatical obedience to a spiritual adviser.

So strong is the fanaticism of the *Spiritual Ladder* that on one occasion an innocent person is punished to make a lesson against materialism where it leads to worthy spiritual training and a good example to others of spiritual training and patience.[5] Other examples of fanaticism abound in this work. The author claims that some people consider eunuchs to be fortunate, since they are spared the temptations of the flesh. He observes that more blessed are those people who become (like) eunuchs by their daily struggle against passion.[6] He speaks with obvious approval of a monk who used a cloth (for protection against temptation) when holding his mother's hand.

We may ask why, if this work is too fanatical even for Granada, did he translate it? One answer is that there is an essential honesty in the work. The author does distinguish clearly between the form and the spirit of the ascetic life. He recognizes the importance (which Granada shares) of adjusting the severity of the rules to the relative experience of the monk living under them. The author does not hold himself to be an example of superiority. He is constantly vigilant for new sins that emerge as by-products of the desperate struggle against old ones. He has good psychological insight into the progress of sin and the struggle against it.

One example in *Spiritual Ladder* which probably appealed to Granada is the analysis of degrees of temptation. The first degree is without sin, since it is involuntary movement, and man cannot prevent such reflex actions. The second degree is delay, which does have an element of sin. The third is consent and depends upon the nature of the temptation to judge its severity. The fourth is the struggle, the amount of sin being related to the success or failure to overcome it. Fifth is the captivity of thought, more or less serious depending upon what duty it replaces. The sixth is the passion which must be purged with penitence or punished in the next life. His conclusion is that the person who avoids the second degree (delay) spares himself much grief.[7] From Granada's original works we can find numerous examples of interest in this kind of numerical listing and analysis, though seldom is the analysis so keen.

The ladder of which Climacus speaks has thirty steps, but there is scant indication that the steps have to be conquered in the order in which they appear. For example, chastity is number fifteen and humility number twenty-five. Both are treated at some length, representing their importance, but their location on the ladder does not seem significant. Granada translated this seventh-century treatise, we may assume, because it is inspiring to those of devout ascetic spirit. It serves as an inspiration to ascetic living and occasionally serves to clarify a point that some struggling sinner might have in the difficult steep road to virtue. Granada softened the rougher edges because he felt that some parts were too starkly austere for his own age.

III   *Granada's Sermons*

It seems to me that a brief attention to Granada's sermons will make a useful addendum to the works already considered. The *Biblioteca de autores españoles* (*Collection of Spanish Writers*) presents thirteen of these sermons, a representative sample.[8] Throughout much of his life Fray Luis was noted for his sermons in which the emphasis was upon the spoken word. Since some of these sermons may have been intended for others to read or use as a model, this sampling may not give as complete a picture as we would like of his spontaneity. This examination of his sermons will, therefore, serve principally to reinforce opinions formed elsewhere.

These sermons, with one exception, form a series appropriate for special occasions. For example, the first three are on Christ's circumcision, the Epiphany, and the Sunday after the Epiphany. A word that seems to be a guide to analyzing these sermons is "consider." This means that the sermon itself is almost like a meditation. He has told us elsewhere that meditation is of two varieties, intellectual and emotional. Obviously these are not mutually exclusive. In most of the sermons there is at least an intellectual or didactic quality in the things that his listener is asked to consider. There is normally also an exhortation to think about the emotional setting. The sermons might be used later as material for meditation.

One of the most beautiful of these sermons is the "Sermon on the Feast of Our Lady's Assumption." Granada naturally directs the listener's thought to the qualities, deeds, and experiences of St. Mary. He begins by picturing the famous Bethany sisters, Martha and Mary. These two friends of Jesus epitomize the practical and contemplative qualities respectively of Christian worship. The Mother of God is described as having the virtues of both and to a greater degree than either. She is contrasted with Lucifer, since she rose from humble beginnings and by humility to occupy her present place in Heaven while he, the brightest star in Heaven, had through pride lost his place and descended to Hell.

Granada directs his listener's attention to her trials as a Mother throughout her Son's life and for twelve years after His ascension, the time understood to be that of Mary's assumption. He almost assumes the authenticity of her assumption; his only defensive comment on that subject is a reference to St. Augustine who said that it is unthinkable that the body from which our Lord received his flesh could ever be handed over to worms.[9] Finally Granada speaks of her unique place in Heaven and of man's privilege and obligation to turn to her in prayer and intercession.

The thirteenth sermon of Granada is different. It is a response to a specific critical event and is more a treatise than a sermon, since it is about six times the length of the other sermons. The event is the fall of María de la Visitación, a nun who had achieved fame as a visionary but who had been exposed as a false mystic. Granada, although already in his eighties, could still see the consternation with which this news was received. If this nun's visitations were proved to be false, how would it affect the credibility of other mystics or religious leaders in general? In a brief summary at the beginning, Granada declares that he will address two points: the credibility of the virtuous as examples of Christian conduct and the morale of the weak, who might think that the road to virtue was too difficult to attain.

The fall of some of those who have achieved places of leadership seems to Fray Luis to be widespread if not inevitable. Among the examples he cited are, Judas Iscariot, all of the sons of Jacob except Joseph, and one of the sons of Noah—presumably Ham. Granada shows sympathy for those who fall and cites examples of repentance. By implication he suggests that one not be shocked or dismayed. There will always be other good examples to emulate, and the power of the Holy Spirit is always here on earth. Fray Luis has a special warning for those who observe one whose fall from grace is formalized by trial by the Inquisition. He warns against fearing the Inquisitors. To him it would be comparable to having the sheep fear the shepherd.

Why does God tempt man in this way? Granada compares it to pottery in the fire—the testing gives strength to those who overcome temptation. The weak cannot gather strength if they are not put to the test. Granada discusses the various temptations in ways that are repetitious of his other works but here focus upon the special problems of persevering in the wake of a bad example. The Holy Communion is his chief medicine against these temptations, and the last part of his sermon is a discussion of the ways to make confession and communion most effective.

The most remarkable aspect of this sermon is that it is Granada's forthright personal reaction. He was indirectly involved in the scandal, since he had defended María de la Visitación against those accusing her of fabricating her visions. He suffered the chagrin of being duped. His own recovery was itself a reinforcement of the words of his sermon.

IV *Rhetoric*

Granada's fame as a preacher and writer may naturally have led to his writing a book in Latin on rhetoric, *Retórica Eclesiastica (Ecclesiastical Rhetoric)*, available in Spanish in the *Collection of Spanish Authors*. Most of Granada's works are directed to the general public, but this one is intended for preachers who want to make their sermons more effective. Compared to his other works, the material deals more with technical matters than with his exhortations, although these are numerous, mostly taken from ancient sources. As usual, he shows care and patience with the organization.

Before discussing the techniques of good rhetoric, Granada reminds his reader that the message is far more important than are the techniques for its presentation. The speaker is expected to be thoroughly acquainted with his subject matter. In this case the speaker should be a preacher, since Fray Luis is not writing this manual for lawyers. The appearance and the reputation of the preacher are important for making the message effective. If the preacher has led an exemplary life, the people will be more inclined to listen and heed. It is important to emphasize that before proceeding to an analysis of technique Granada makes sure that his ultimate purpose, bringing people to God, is foremost in the mind of his reader. His assumption is that if the end is thoroughly grasped and understood, the application of the means cannot distort it.

Granada's training in rhetoric is based largely upon Aristotle, Cicero, and Quintilian, but he makes a distinction from the beginning that clarifies his relationship to the ancient mentors. They taught the art of dialectics, a form of applied reasoning, an exercise in intellectual skill where one speaker may be matching wits with another. Granada points out that his reader will be trying to move the general public and so an emotional approach rather than a rational one should normally be stressed.

Fray Luis defines, explains, and illustrates the various terms such as syllogism, dilemma, and sentence (aphorism). His illustrations come from biblical, classical, and patristic sources. These terms, in which he often uses both the Latin and Greek words, may subconsciously show his erudition, though Granada warns the reader against using language designed to flaunt erudition rather than to present the message clearly and persuasively. More important to him, however, is to see that a sermon is organized in such a way as to consider equally the message and the people who are to receive it.

Let a few illustrations serve to indicate Granada's thinking in the preparation of this work. Since he is aware that the preacher is likely to take his source material in Latin and address the people in the vernacular, he advises the preacher to be aware of the subtleties of language so that he will, on the one hand, avoid the stilted quality of a literal rendering of the Latin message in Spanish (or Portuguese) and, at the other extreme, avoid a bombastic style if the preacher tries to display linguistic virtuosity. One rather striking analogy included in Granada's illustrative material tells of a painter who, by careful labor, paints a beautiful picture. An inferior painter comes along, takes his brush, and makes some substantial changes in the other man's work. The reader is asked to consider the first painter's feelings. By this analogy the first painter is God, who has fashioned the face of a woman; the second is the woman herself who has applied makeup.

Granada describes various types of sermons and how to organize them and warns the preacher against specializing in the one in which he has the greatest interest or skill to the exclusion of other necessary types. He openly advocates exaggeration of illustrative material to try to describe the values of virtue or the harm of vice. This form of exaggeration would of course not distort the religious truths that he is advocating but simply help to dramatize them.

Granada's emphasis is first, on the knowledge and practice of the truth, second, on the proper organization of a sermon so that the effect upon the hearer is clarified and strengthened and third, on the application of eloquence so that the voice can be an effective instrument for conveying the message. He likes beautiful words for beauty's sake, but, in an analogy, he warns that even a golden key is of limited value if it does not unlock anything.

Granada is aware that a person can study carefully the many figures of speech and other elements of oral eloquence, and prepare a sermon bearing in mind the need for using them to embellish the sermon, with the lamentable result that the message itself can be lost in the process. He advises extensive reading and attention to useful examples. He insists upon careful organization so that the sermon will have a solid structure, and he warns that figures of speech and other rhetorical devices be used with measure. He advises careful attention to the nature of the congregation to present a sermon appropriate for them. He generally advises naturalness in the preparation and delivery of a sermon. The teacher can hardly do more; the innate skill of the performer must take over.

The best analysis of the rhetoric of Granada as a theoretical science and as an applied art is Rebecca Switzer's *The Ciceronian Style in Fray Luis de Granada*.[10] In addition to analyzing the uses of rhetoric Miss Switzer places the subject of style in its historical setting and claims for Granada considerable influence in the formation and style of the Spanish language. She agrees that Granada imitated Cicero in the best possible sense by copying his attitude toward style rather than imitating specific figures of speech and syntactical arrangements. Thus Granada avoided the sins against style of slavish imitation, bombastic language, stilted speech, or obscure expression.

CHAPTER 7

Granada's Critics

A writer as widely read as Fray Luis de Granada has attracted relatively little attention from the critics. The public has read his works for the very reason that he intended them to be read—spiritual guidance and uplift, but the critics, with scattered exceptions, have preferred to treat those religious writers who seemed to offer greater poetic talent or a stronger sense of the mystical inspiration. For a consideration of those who have treated Granada I prefer to introduce them in three categories: Granada's Dominican defenders, the critics specializing in mystical writings, and the miscellaneous ones, bearing in mind that the last category contains some of the most important.

I *The Dominican Defenders*

Father Justo Cuervo is the most significant name in scholarship relating to Granada. He has compiled an edition of Granada's *Obras* (*Works*) in fourteen volumes.[1] He has written what is apparently the definitive biography.[2] He has commented in special works on areas where he considers that Granada's interests are at stake. One of these concerns Fray Luis and the Inquisition.[3] Here he refers to the *Index* of 1559, the only restriction by the Inquisition of Granada's literary activity.

Father Cuervo makes the following points in this article: The Inquisition did not move against Granada personally at any time, a point which is quite significant when one considers how severely others have been treated, especially during that time. The matter found objectionable by the Inquisition consisted of some passages in the *Book of Prayer and Meditation* which seemed to them to recall the *alumbrado* quality and thus seemed heterodox to these censors. Cuervo reports that Granada patiently revised the book to remove passages found objectionable and that permission to print again came from the pope while he was at Trent. Cuervo emphasizes that Granada was a great defender of the Inquisition. This article says virtually nothing about the *Guide for Sinners,* which was also banned. Granada's revision of this book was so thorough that the problems with the Inquisition must have formed only a minor part of his motivation for a second version. The revised version is much longer even though large sections of the first version were removed.

Father Cuervo seemed to have a stronger interest in another area of Granada's scholarship. Appended to Cuervo's biography of Granada, the Dominican apologist has written a thorough study, *Fray Luis de Granada, verdadero y único autor del "Libro de la oración"* (*Fray Luis de Granada, True and Sole Author of the "Book of Prayer"*). His purpose was to refute assertions that Fray Luis had taken a treatise on prayer by San Pedro de Alcántara and amplified it in composing his book. Cuervo keeps his readers abreast of a running polemic with a Franciscan journal *El eco.* Arguments concern in part the number of years prior to publication that the respective works circulated in manuscript. Cuervo's claim is that Granada's work was composed at an earlier date, much earlier in fact, and that San Pedro made a compendium of it. A part of the dispute involves the dating of Granada's arrival at Scala Coeli (see biography), the abandoned convent that he was to revive. If, as Padre Cuervo asserts, Granada wrote his book in the 1530s, there was no way that it could have been an enlargement of Alcántara's treatise. Cuervo further asserts that if Granada had started with Alcántara's work and enlarged it, he would have said so. There is no effort on either side accusing either author of plagiarism.

Cuervo has an interesting hypothesis for the timing of the publication of San Pedro's treatise. In 1559, Granada's *Book of Prayer and Meditation* was placed on the *Index*—as noted above. Cuervo thinks that while Granada was revising the work to remove the material to which the Inquisition had objected, San Pedro made his compendium of it to help fill the void. This is plausible, since the treatise in question was published in 1560. Disinterested critics such as E. Allison Peers agree with Cuervo concerning the originality of Granada's work, but wish to restore some of the credit to San Pedro de Alcántara for originality in his own publication.[4]

Father Máximo Llaneza is the successor to Padre Cuervo as chief Granadan scholar among the Dominicans. He has written a monumental bibliography comprising four large volumes.[5] Even so, its scope is limited. It treats principally editions of Granada's works. It is only in a supplement that he lists some biographies of Fray Luis and eulogies of his works. There is no critical study listed. It is a valuable tool for locating the editions of Granada's works in the libraries and bookstores of the world, somewhat outdated now with the passage of a half-century. Its very size speaks eloquently of Granada's continued popularity down through the ages. It is also significant for the sporadic comments of the bibliographer, most of which are defenses of Granada, written with a zeal and an indignation that suggest comparing his statements with those of scholars with a more objective point of view. Particularly do we object to his including editions of the work of San Pedro de Alcántara, cited above, among those of Granada.

While we are forced to conclude that Llaneza was often overzealous in Granada's cause, he was certainly modest enough about his own contributions to Granadan scholarship. In his introduction, he pays tribute to Father Cuervo as the inspirer and initiator of the task, which death prevented him from completing. He credits the Dominican provincial, Father Luis Getino, with organizing the study and underwriting its publication. It is evident, however, that Llaneza is the one who executed the task and should be given entire credit for a work whose preparation took him on trips throughout Europe and required meticulous attention for several years.

The contributions of Father Luis Getino to Granadan scholarship go beyond those acknowledged in the previous paragraph. He defended Granada in another polemic, this time against the Jesuits. In 1658, the Jesuit Juan Eusebio Nieremberg wrote an excellent translation of the *Contemptus mundi*. This edition largely (though not completely) replaced Granada's own translation. Getino claimed that what Nieremberg did was to retouch Granada's translation to remove the archaisms of a century of linguistic evolution. He compares samples of the two translations and adds:

It would not be strange for Father Nieremberg to publish a version of Kempis, in spite of the very polished edition of Granada, because a work finished in 1536 would need in 1650 the retouches that the new transformation of our language demanded. Nieremberg could have written as well as any a new version for his time.

He could have done it, but he didn't; he offered us the very version of Granada retouched by him. What is strange isn't that either, but that it should be published and be known as Father Nieremberg's when it should be called a work translated by Granada and amended by Nieremberg.

The passage quoted is Getino's edition of Kempis *Imitación de Cristo* (*Imitation of Christ*), translated by Granada and modernized by Getino.[6] That Father Nieremberg consulted Granada's translation, there can be little doubt. That his translation should or should not be called a new one is a matter of opinion. Half of the corrections were, by Getino's own admission, unnecessary[7] and therefore could have resulted from Nieremberg's effort to display his own style. It seems to us that Nieremberg made the work thoroughly his own and was justified in calling the translation a new one. More important to us than Father Getino's assertions about the Nieremberg translation is his own modern version of Granada's translation, cited above. Here indeed is a version which is basically the version of Granada. Only a few words have been given modern spellings; all of Granada's variations have been preserved. This edition, for a general reading public, is convincing evidence that Granada's translation is a dependable and readable one even today.

II *Granada's Mysticism*

Students of Spanish literature, on reaching the subject of the Spanish mystics, traditionally have been taught to cite Paul Rousselot's *Les mystiques espagnols* (*The Spanish Mystics*)[8] and E. Allison Peers' *Studies of the Spanish Mystics*,[9] both of whom treat Granada extensively. A word of caution is in order with respect to Rousselot's analysis of Granada. His study appeared before the important studies by Father Cuervo, cited above, and by Bataillon.[10] Therefore, he lacked a number of facts now available. In particular his views of Granada and the Inquisition need updating.

Rousselot, however, was a fine scholar, possessed of excellent insight. Instead of trying to measure the mysticism in Granada as a separate phenomenon, he measures the man: the mystic, the ascetic, the rational scholar, the inspired preacher, the beloved teacher, in short, the integrated personality. Some of Rousselot's expressions are worth quoting: "To preach, to write, to direct souls, such was his life and his vocation; simple monk, composer of sermons, theologian, he felt more at home serving the church, and where necessary defending it, than rising to higher positions."[11]

Rousselot follows this with a contrast between Granada's positive reform and the autos-da-fé protecting orthodoxy. Later, analyzing Granada's eclecticism, he carefully portrays it in connection with Plato and Aristotle and the Dominican St. Thomas Aquinas:

He is not as profound as Bossuet in his *elevaciones*, but he is more moving because he is mystical. More Platonic than the great Bishop of Meaux, although less so than Fenelon, since, although Dominican and consequently Thomistic, he follows the Academy with greater pleasure than the Lyceum and feels for Plato a true sympathy which St. Thomas did not experience to the same degree, bearing in mind that St. Thomas could not have known Plato as well as he did.[12]

It is natural for Rousselot, a Frenchman, to cite the conservative French theologian Bossuet, Bishop of Meaux, and the liberal Fenelon for his examples. He continues by pointing out that Granada, despite his affinity for Plato, did not derive his mysticism from Platonic philosophy. There is a paradox in all this that Rousselot seemed fully to understand. Because of Granada's training, he seems to be a very complex individual; placed in the middle of all the religious controversies, he did not seem to belong to any camp. On the other hand, he was a very simple person because of his lack of personal ambition and because of his hesitancy to think for himself—having so many authorities he could cite.

E. Allison Peers is primarily concerned with mysticism as a literary art or as an artistically expressed distillation of mysticism's essence. As such, asceticism, theology, didactic literature, and moral philosophy are outside the realm that he has decided to write about. In common with most orthodox students of mysticism, Peers sees the orderly progression of the mystic to the higher forms, whether expressed in the symbol of the ascent of a symbolic mountain or as delving ever deeper into the inner mansions of the soul. He recognizes Granada as primarily an ascetic. He virtually admits that Granada as a mystic disappoints him:

Fray Luis does not distinguish carefully between the various mystic states, and consequently gives no clear idea of the mystic's progress. We find him writing suddenly of the Unitive Life, then descending to the level of vocal prayer, then passing to a state which he describes as "contemplation," the nature of which seems to be similar to Osuna's "Prayer of Recollection" or St. Teresa's "Prayer of Quiet."[13]

Nevertheless, Peers considers Fray Luis among the more important Spanish mystics after St. Theresa and St. John of the Cross. He
quotes numerous passages of beautiful mystic inspiration from different Granada books. He attributes the lack of description of sustained and heightened mystical activity first to Granada's being
primarily an ascetic and second to his writing for a broad public
rather than a smaller group of mystics, and concludes that he is a
mystic at heart. Peers also presents the view that if Granada were
writing expressly for a group of mystics he would have written in a
more personal way. Among the passages which Peers quotes is this
one taken from the *Book of Prayer and Meditation:*

There are others who have greater freedom, and in these God closes the
vein of speculation, and opens that of affection, to the end that the understanding may be calmed and stilled, and the will may take its rest and
delight in God alone, being occupied wholly in the love and fruition of its
supreme Good. This is the most perfect state of contemplation, and to this
we must ever aspire.[14]

We have seen, and Peers implicitly bears it out, that Granada was
not interested in mapping the ascent of Mount Carmel. He wished
mainly to help his fellow man serve God, and he loved to use the
inspiring examples of holy men and women. He almost never in-
jected his own experience into his narrative. He looked upon
spiritual consolations—one form of mystical experience—with some
concern lest they become an end in themselves. It seems to me that
our most plausible assumption is that a man so cautious never
clearly experienced those higher mystical states so clearly de-
lineated by St. Theresa and St. John of the Cross. Otherwise, I
believe that Granada would have felt compelled to use his own
experience as a Christian witness. However, I will gladly second
Peers's final statement:

He is filled with the true mystical spirit of the great doctors whose names
are ever on his lips, and for all that he seems to neglect the higher slopes of
Carmel, we feel that, while he is busy guiding others on the lower slopes,
he feels rest and refreshment in constantly looking and pointing upward to
the summit.[15]

III   *Other Critics*

Marcel Bataillon, in his article "De Savonarole à Louis de Granade,"[16] analyzes succinctly the influence of Savonarola on Granada but, at the same time, puts into perspective the full picture of the intra-Catholic controversy of the age. He addresses himself first to the question, how did the ideas of Savonarola reach Granada? Implied in this question is that the ideas of a man beheaded for rebellion against the pope would not spread freely through Christendom. A part of his answer is simply that Savonarola and Granada were both Dominicans.

The influence mentioned here is upon Granada's *Book of Prayer and Meditation* and deals with certain aspects of spirituality. Bataillon admits that a simplified analysis of the Dominican order's contributions to Catholic progress tends to stress dogma rather than spirituality, but he points out that this tendency does not reach monolithic proportions. In fact, in the battle that seemed to be emerging in Spain in the middle of the sixteenth century, the leading representative of the dogma and spirituality factions, Melchor Cano and Bartolomé Carranza respectively, were both Dominicans. There was, therefore, no reason before 1559 (the year of Valdés's *Index*) for Granada not to utilize anything written by Savonarola that he thought useful.[17]

The influence of Savonarola upon Granada cited by Bataillon focuses upon two areas in particular: the question of the relationship between vocal and mental prayer and the question of whether the guidelines for prayer should be different for cleric and layman. Most specifically, in the first version of the *Book of Prayer and Meditation* Granada, adapting Savonarola, uses two parables or analogies for vocal prayer. One is that it is like a medicine that one should take until he is well enough spiritually to utilize mental prayer. The other is a comparison with a sailor who relaxes his vigil somewhat when his ship is safely in harbor. The implication is that vocal prayer is of special importance when one is in difficulty in trying to use mental prayer, but that once a person achieves the concentration necessary for mental prayer, the vocal prayer has diminished importance. Bataillon points out that these two analogies were dropped in the revised version but he proclaims, perhaps with some pride, that Granada did not retreat at all in the question of the right and appropriateness of the use of mental prayer by those who have not taken monastic vows.

I think it should be pointed out here, though I cannot read this into Bataillon's analysis, that Granada's decision not to use Savonarola's analogy of medicine or of the sailor probably came from his realization that using it was inconsistent with his own views as well as those of the Inquisition. Such an analogy could be the first step to the complete abandonment of vocal prayer and thus contrary to Granada's concept of the balanced program.[18] Certainly one highly significant part of Bataillon's message in this article is his view of the use which Granada makes of his borrowed material. He applies it specifically to the passages taken from Savonarola, but it could be applied to all of Fray Luis's adaptations of other writers:

By these comparisons one does not intend in the slightest to diminish the importance of Luis de Granada. He succeeded in drawing out in every sense the thought of his predecessor in developing all the riches with an ingenuity which is a creation in his own manner. It is not to be doubted, however, that Savonarola's sermon served as a text for his meditations as much as the text of Luke itself; without him the *Book of Prayer* would not have received this rich coronation.[19]

Bataillon also deals often with Granada in his work, *Erasme et l'Espagne (Erasmus and Spain)*, cited above. The French scholar sees the history of religion in Spain's sixteenth century as a struggle between pro- and anti-Erasmus forces, and sees a significant role for Granada in this struggle. The nature of this controversy, slightly oversimplified, is illustrated by Erasmus's objection to the belief that formal prayer has an objective power, irrespective of the spirit in which it is expressed. Why, he might ask, should ten paternosters be ten times as effective as one would be? He describes such thinking as pharisaical because the Pharisees had been accused of following the letter of the law without any sense of charity behind it.

On the other side of the coin, the anti-Erasmus forces saw a danger in placing complete faith in the spirit of prayer, which if carried to an extreme would make the services of the Church unnecessary. Each group was in danger of excessive spiritual pride. Bataillon studies carefully the intertwining of politics and theology in the development of this struggle.

As we know, Lutheranism never reached Spain in force, but its main effect there was to tempt the anti-Erasmus group to equate the ideas of Erasmus with those of Luther. Thus friends and followers of Erasmus, who had no thought of splitting with the Church, found themselves accused of heresy. As Lutheranism and other Protestant sects spread in the North, fear of heresy increased in Spain, and the persecution of the Erasmian ideal and of Erasmists reached its zenith in the early years of Phillip II's reign.

The view that I have held of Fray Luis and religious politics is that he is so otherworldly that he is not only impervious to such political infighting, but that he is almost oblivious of its existence. Obviously, that cannot be completely true and Bataillon makes no such assumption. For him, Granada is on the side of Erasmus and consciously so.

There are several respects in which Granada obviously sides with Erasmus. First, he believed in writing religious treatises for the benefit of the common man. He spent the last thirty years of his life trying to make it possible for the man who did not know Latin to have all of the spiritual reading that he needed. Second, as we have seen with Savonarola, he defended mental prayer as a proper religious exercise for anyone. He expressed strongly the view that the form without the spirit was of little value. Bataillon seems to stress these affinities.

There are other important aspects in which Granada seems to be different from Erasmus. Granada did not seem to enjoy a religious polemic as an intellectual exercise. One might even say that for him the use of the intellect for its own sake was a form of aberration from its proper purpose to serve God. Granada was not worried about form and ritual in itself. He loathed a tepid performance but did not see form as a hindrance to the working of the spirit. For him, the routine practice of religious exercises was a safeguard in keeping the soul occupied in serving God. Bataillon does not deny this contrast but certainly does not stress it.

One might conclude that an important reason for Bataillon's interest in Granada expressed in his book on Erasmus in Spain was that Granada was such a well-known conservative. Since Bataillon is openly pro-Erasmus, for the scholar from Rotterdam to have Granada in his camp suggests how extreme the anti-Erasmus position could become at times. Bataillon has twenty-five references to Granada, some extending over several pages. This work is a monument of Spanish literary criticism, broad, deep, and scholarly.

Dámaso Alonso, the famous poet and critic, impressed by Bataillon's scholarship, has also considered the influence of Erasmus upon Granada.[20] Alonso readily accepts the idea that Erasmus influenced Granada, but he observes that the identity of concepts noticed by

Bataillon, while a strong indication, was not a strict proof of the direct influence of Erasmus upon Granada. Since Erasmus is to a large extent interpreting St. Paul's views on the spirit of Christianity, and since others in his time were interpreting a similar spirituality, this influence could have been indirect.

Alonso himself supplies the direct verbal evidence. He discovered two passages which indicated to him that Granada had used a translation of Erasmus's *Enquiridion*. One of these is in the 1556 edition of *Sinner's Guide*, the other in the revised (1567) edition of the same work and a completely different passage.[21] Alonso makes clear that he does not see Granada as risking deviation from the orthodox. Granada does not name Erasmus in these citations or anywhere else (his tendency is to cite names honored by centuries but to refer to any of his near contemporaries simply as "a doctor"); to do so would possibly be indiscreet, but Alonso's citations do emphasize the idea that Granada held no fear of the Inquisition.

Fidel de Ros discusses the influence of the Northern Mystics on Fray Luis de Granada.[22] He is well aware of the wide influences upon Granada from classical and Christian sources through the ages and of Granada's scrupulous care in citing sources for references utilized. He is therefore understandably curious as he uncovers numerous examples of materials translated or virtually copied without identification of the citation. He points out a score of adaptations of materials from the writings of Louis de Blois (1506–1566), a contemporary of Granada who began his writing career somewhat earlier than Fray Luis. A large percentage of these borrowings are used in the original edition of *Sinner's Guide* (the edition placed on the *Index* of 1559). Ros also points to material taken from the Pseudo Tauler,[23] used in the morning meditation series of the *Book of Prayer and Meditation*. Finally, Fidel de Ros calls attention to Granada's use of extracts from the works of Herp.[24] His main purpose in calling attention to these influences is simply to let scholars know of their existence and to complement the Bataillon article on Savonarola and Granada. He does observe that apparently Granada was more cautious after 1559 in the matter of citing authors close in time to his own works.

It is interesting and helpful to accumulate these examples of Granada's use of unidentified writers (Fidel de Ros is silent on Erasmus). It shows that Granada was well acquainted with the Northern mystic tradition in other ways than through Kempis. Fidel de Ros does not try to weigh this influence by suggesting that it changed the point of view of Granada. He does point out that a posited early dating of the composition of the *Book of Prayer and Meditation* is wrong, at least to the extent that the demonstrated influence of Pseudo Tauler could not have antedated 1548, and therefore the work would at least have suffered revision after that date.

José Martínez Ruiz (Azorín) wrote a little book called *Los dos Luises*. [25] One Louis was Fray Luis de Granada, the other, Fray Luis de León. The idea is flattering to Granada, since León is one of the most sensitive poets, one of the most intellectual scholars, and one of the most dynamic personalities in the history of Spanish religious literature. When Azorín writes an essay about a writer from the past, the result is more a creative work of literature itself than a literary analysis, but Azorín does bring out, in his unique way, the salient features of the author in question or a vivid evocation of the setting in which he writes. One important consideration of this book is the fact that Azorín undertook it. The sophisticated writer of the twentieth century is not likely to linger long upon the writings of an unsophisticated, austere, ascetic monk of the sixteenth century. One would suspect the result to be the benign patronizing attitude which the urbane take when they seek pristine simplicity in an earlier age or a more rustic setting.

If such is the case, Azorín surprises us. Perhaps we should say Granada surprises him. He expected to find Granada wordy and bombastic; he found instead a model of simple prose style. His eloquence is in his thought more than in his choice of words; the love emanating from his heart seems to have no need to tarry while the words to express it are pondered. Azorín liked Granada's love of nature. He considered it rare for a preromantic writer to consider nature as something more than the background or setting for his story. He expressed admiration that Granada could walk among the rich and powerful, maintaining his dignified poverty and not censuring extravagance. He singled out Granada's descriptions of the stupidity of war—descriptions which contained no hint that war could be just or righteous. He was impressed by Granada's thoughts on Mary Magdalene and the importance of genuine repentance. Perhaps for Azorín the culmination of Granada's inspiration is his vision of Heaven. He quotes Granada's words. Unfortunately they must be translated only approximately here.

Will we enjoy Heaven with our senses? What will have become of our organs of corporeal apprehension? [These words are Azorín's introducing Granada's answer] "Each one will have his unique joy and glory. The eyes renewed and clarified above the light of the sun will see those royal palaces, those glorious [heavenly] bodies and fields of beauty, with other infinite things that there will be to see. The ears will always hear that music of such softness, that a single voice will suffice to put to sleep all the hearts of the world. The sense of smell will be recreated with such soft odors, not vaporous things as here, but proportioned to the glory there. And thus the pleasure will be filled with incredible savor and sweetness, not to sustain life but for the fulfillment of all glory."[26]

Azorín also wrote about Granada in *De Granada a Castelar*,[27] a study of style in writing. Azorín here shows the significant relation between the content and the vehicle, the importance of reading and writing to develop an oratorical style, and the place of Granada in the formation of Spanish ideas of clarity in the development of style. Thus Azorín shows his genuine admiration for Granada, his wish to revive his name, especially since Granada is among those who helped form the Spanish written language in the early years of Spanish printing. Apparently few of his sophisticated friends shared this enthusiasm.

CHAPTER 8

Recapitulation

O UR goal has been to try to evaluate the significance of Fray Luis de Granada in sixteenth-century Spanish letters. The aim of most writers is to compose in such a way as to attract the interest of regular readers and to earn the esteem of critics. Therefore, with the evaluation of most writers the task of the critic is to determine how well the writer has accomplished his goals. Fray Luis's goal was to convert the theological wisdom which he had studied to a simple practical guide for living for the monk or layman who had no special expertise but who wished to follow the teaching of the church. Since our criteria concern literary values while Granada's goal is didactic efficiency, the things that interest us are tangential features of his writings. Despite the natural desire to judge a man by what he was trying to do, we must evaluate Granada according to our criteria rather than his.

Since Granada's goals are obviously not our goals, we tend to become a little impatient with him, feeling that he had the talent to do a better job of fulfilling our criteria. We share Azorín's admiration for Granada's direct simple language, but after admiring his clarity we wish he had confined his efforts to one clear expression of his idea instead of exercising the teacher's penchant for drill. We recognize with Peers his deep understanding of mysticism; yet we also share with Peers a feeling that Granada has treated what seems to us a sublime religious phenomenon in the same context as an everyday religious experience. We see a man who, like Erasmus, seemed capable of leading men from medieval into modern ways of thinking but who seemed to hold back from this type of leadership. Granada was both prolific and verbose. How we wish he had been able (or willing) to give us the wine of his wisdom distilled into one small volume that we could understand and appreciate quickly!

It seems to me that we should begin to understand Granada's

significance by placing him in the context of the religious world of Spain's sixteenth century. He was one of five great Spanish religious figures of that age. One of these, St. Ignatius of Loyola, although an influential writer, achieved his fame largely as founder of the Jesuits. The other four were mainly considered as writers, although all were active in the religious life. Their age was the age of the breakdown of Europe's religious unity, and they helped Spain to remain staunchly Catholic while upholding principles which spawned the Protestant Reformation elsewhere. Fray Luis de Granada was the oldest of these four and the one who experienced least difficulty from religious controversy. Perhaps in part because of controversy, the other three (St. Theresa, Fray Luis de León, and St. John of the Cross) seem to have made deeper impressions upon our age, but chronologically at least, Granada was the leader, and his steadfastness and evenhandedness must have been most influential.

Fray Luis was fitted for his life as leader and diplomat by being given, at a relatively early age, the task of leading Scala Coeli, a convent that had been virtually abandoned but was being revived. Later he became provincial for the Dominican order in Portugal. He served well in both capacities, but the real tests of his diplomacy came in less formal ways. In his middle years he wrote many books while remaining complaisant even while knowing that every word would be examined critically and with an attitude of suspicion of heterodoxy. Later, he served the Portuguese crown in the midst of increasing antipathy between Spain and Portugal. Finally, after the Spanish takeover, he did what he could to preserve a spirit of equanimity among Portuguese Dominicans.

Granada's education seemed to have equipped him well, not only for writing his books but also for living in an age in which religion and politics became so intermingled. San Gregorio at Valladolid introduced him to the diverse points of view of Greek philosophers and of Christian religious writers. We may wonder what his thoughts were as he was completing this education. He studied the Bible carefully and apparently accepted readily symbolic, analogical, and prophetic interpretations of many points where literal interpretation would present difficulties or would be meaningless from a religious point of view. He also studied and admired Plato and Aristotle, St. Augustine and St. Thomas Aquinas. Did he see any irreconcilable differences? If, as Rousselot contends, Granada had a natural leaning toward Plato, and consequently St. Augustine, was he ever troubled by views of a different spirit expressed by the Dominican theologian Aquinas? He even quotes on occasion from Scotus. From Granada's writings all those cited seem to be of indisputable authority and no views openly conflict with any others. In fact, Granada's sources are so numerous and so diverse that a scholar would be mad to try to analyze them.[1]

And what of Granada's teachers? Melchor Cano and Bartolomé Carranza held irreconcilable views which led to the imprisonment of the latter by the Inquisition. Was Granada aware of this antipathy as he learned from them? He must have been aware of these differences and he must have been troubled by them, but from his writings and from his actions we see no bedfellows that he finds strange.

We can see several steps that Granada took to avoid the clash of ideas. In the first place he was obviously dedicated to explaining the Catholic faith and the ascetic way of life to those who wished guidance for living rather than those who sought points in competitive logic. Second, he was very much aware that there are places in which rational explanation falters and faith in revealed truth must take over. For example, he asks his reader to accept on faith the concept of the Trinity and not to speculate about it. In this connection he can use the philosophers any way he chooses. If he thinks they are right, he can comment upon their thoughts, giving praise to their natural reason. If he thinks they are wrong, he can still comment favorably upon their noble spirit and lament their lack of divine Revelation to guide them.

Since Granada seemed so skillful in avoiding controversial topics in a controversial age and environment, it is difficult to show how he faced a confrontation head-on. Assuming that these were inevitable I am asking the reader to permit me for a moment to indulge in speculative imagining, and I shall try to suggest what I believe would have been his attitude and manner. Let us assume that Granada was confronted with arguments for a basic Lutheran contention: justification by grace through faith alone versus a Catholic concept of the equally basic importance of faith and works to obtain salvation through grace. I am assuming that by works one means, partly if not principally, performance of church rituals, recitation of prescribed prayers, attendance at religious services, and gifts to the church. Granada, as a good Catholic, would start with the doctrine of his church and marshall arguments to support it. He would of course agree that faith and works are twin pillars in salvation's formula. He would not only admit but also emphasize that a mechanical observance of works is not pleasing to God. "Are indulgences wrong?" he might be asked.[2] I believe that he would agree that for indulgences to be effective the spirit has to be a spirit of contrition. He would not admit, however, that the practice itself tends to corrupt and would refuse to speculate about any value that a performance might have if not indulged in with a proper spirit. This is not a compromise; it is rather the refusal to acknowledge the existence of a problem. It was an admirable spirit, but it was not the spirit of the times.

For many writers it is possible to show that their biographies hold the key to the nature of their works. By observing the effect of strong emotion at critical moments of a man's life, one can show what motivated a poem, the theme of a novel, or perhaps a religious conversion or time of dedication. There seems little for an amateur psychologist to work with to explain crises in Granada's life, for apparently there were no dramatic changes. He presumably felt the call to the cloister quite early, perhaps before he was old enough to consider the emotional meaning of the vows of obedience, poverty, and chastity. The poverty of the cloister could hardly have been more severe than that experienced by this son of a widow who was a laundress. We know of no temptation in Granada's life which would have made him wonder, even momentarily, whether he should have become a monk. After his "graduate" education at San Gregorio, he seemed to have chosen the call of the preacher rather than that of the scholar. He preferred associating with and teaching the average man rather than seeking high office or an academic atmosphere.

Despite his obvious piety, it is easy to sense that Granada has his human side. There seems to be no hatred in him, but at least he seems capable of relaxing his ascetic vigil from time to time, even if his biographers give us no clues as to what his peccadillos were. I wonder about Granada's sense of humor. He seems to be a thoroughly serious man, but on rare occasions he will tell a story whose major thrust seems to be a hearty laugh. For example, he tells of the providence of God in giving eagles the intelligence or instinct to cope with the special problem of extracting food from a tortoise which is protected under his shell. According to Granada the eagle will drop the tortoise from a height onto a rock to smash his shell. He reports that the poet Aschylus was mistaken by an eagle for a rock. The eagle dropped his tortoise onto the bald pate and killed the old dramatist.[3]

As Granada grew older he changed only by a slow mellowing. One can see it in his parade of books. First is his translation of the *Imitation of Christ* with the morbid fear of worldliness that it manifests. Next is the *Book of Prayer and Meditation* where he uses almost melodramatic language to show the contrast between worldliness and Christ. Following this is the *Sinner's Guide* which teaches a rigid austerity, but in a calmer tone. Finally there is the *Introduction to the Symbol of Faith* in which he presents reasoned arguments for the Christian faith and can forget about sin and temptation as he is absorbed in considering God's providence through nature and through the inspiration of saints and martyrs.

There is no fundamental change in Granada as he grows older, but rather a gradual change in emphasis. If serenity is a virtue, surely we must praise a man who acquired it through the difficult years of religious disputes that led to the Inquisition's *Index* of 1559 and to the long and not altogether successful Council of Trent. Nor did he lose any of this serenity as, growing to an age in which most men retire, he maintained a position as an influential Spaniard in Portugal when the Portuguese were suffering such helpless anguish.

It is not possible to read any one of Granada's books and claim to know the man. His first major work, the *Book of Prayer and Meditation,* is precisely what the title says. Granada maintains that the two words, prayer and meditation, are synonyms and are complementary, since the same spirit should govern both. He thus tries to bridge the gap between those who urge meditation as a higher form of prayer and those who think it is a dangerous form when practiced by people not thoroughly disciplined in religious service. It pleases the Erasmists to the extent that it stresses spirit over form. It disturbs the orthodox to the extent that it seems to free the spirit from the form. While Granada may occasionally appear to transcend the form, he is so careful to stress the importance of routine and discipline and so vigilant toward the danger of spiritual pride that only the most fearful and suspicious can see the *alumbrado* in his works.

Generally regarded as Granada's masterpiece is his *Sinner's Guide.* Here he examines virtues and vices: how to acquire and preserve virtues and how to avoid or overcome vices. It has had the greatest appeal among his books, because the average Christian can take advantage of the many practical suggestions. It is perhaps the best written, especially since it was thoroughly reconstructed between the first and second versions. Granada balances the ideas of good works and devotion as equally acceptable to God and suggests that an individual stress the one that appeals most to him without envying a person who may be more capable in the other. Lofty ideals are presented in a way to be effective pedagogically and psychologically.

The *Memorial of the Christian Life* and its sequel, the *Additions*, contain little that is basic which is not found in the other two books. Their value to us is mainly that one can see here a sense of hierarchy in the intensity of Christian living. Granada does suggest here that there is a certain minimum standard which he believes that Christ asks, but that some may want to go beyond this minimum in devotion, spurred by a spirit of love. It gives him an opportunity to consider the more mystical aspects of love without dwelling upon the contrasting notes of sin and hate.

The most intellectual of the works is Granada's *Introduction to the Symbol of Faith*. This is the only place in which he shows his concern for the conversion of people from other faiths, and, by implication, the preservation of the faith of those born to Catholicism. His concern about faith is not the establishment of a precisely worded creed which can be memorized and recited periodically, but rather the relationship between faith and life. He shows the beauty and order of the Creation, the irrepressible constancy of the Christian martyrs, and the explanation of the Old and New Testaments with the Old Testament described as the prophesy and promise, and the New Testament as the fulfillment. It severely warns the Jews who do not see the New Testament as the fulfillment of their own prophesies but he does not suggest that an individual Jew has upon his soul the weight of his race's alleged apostasy.

In general, eclecticism is the chief feature of Granada's writings. While some religious leaders may specialize in a branch of theology, others stimulate evangelical activity, advocate greater charity or a more ascetic life, Granada prefers the balanced approach. He is intellectual enough for the theologian, Spartan enough for the ascetic, zealous enough for the preacher, and gracious enough to bring out the best in all.

Three special areas highlight Granada's contribution to Spanish letters and give scholars a specialized interest in him. First, let us mention his influence upon style. He quite early recognized that eloquence was an effective weapon to assist logic and that moving men's hearts was as important as instructing their minds. He wrote as a preacher would speak, and, important for its influence upon the language, he wrote at a time when Castilian was consolidating its linguistic hegemony in Spain, edging out Latin as the written language as it already had its sister dialects in the spoken. His writings are a model for eloquence with simplicity and clarity, a model for his successors, both clerical and secular.

Second is his love of nature. He combined the nature that he studied in books with the nature that he observed. He saw science as a manifestation of the mind of God, beautiful, orderly. eternal. Nature was life and taught man about life. It gave him a sense of the unity of Heaven and earth. It showed him the harmony between beauty and truth. He was a little too medieval to see it as the harmony of the flesh and the spirit, but he centered man in nature far more than most of his contemporaries did.

Finally, there is Granada's mysticism. Of course, one studying Spanish mysticism would naturally think first of the Carmelite saints, Theresa and John of the Cross. When one does turn to Granada, he discovers that all too often his mystical thoughts are not organized. They occur sporadically in his works, especially in his treatise on prayer. Many of his most inspiring thoughts are quotations from other writers. When he writes about mysticism it is not about his personal experiences. He does show, however, that his mind and heart are attuned to an appreciation of mystical experiences and thoughts. The fact that his mystical expressions are often not original does not keep them from being inspiring. Perhaps his main contribution, however, is in showing us that mysticism is only a part of religion. It is a beautiful thing, but like all beautiful things, it can be cherished for the wrong reasons. Mysticism is a road to God, but not the only one. Granada puts it into perspective along with all other aspects of man's religious experience. The nature of Granada's work suggests that his relatively modest place in the history of Spanish mysticism stems, not from his loving God less, relative to the other mystics, but to his loving mankind more.

The value of Granada's work is severely limited for certain types of critical readers. For some he was too inclined to accept the prevailing authority, whether scientific or theological, and was therefore not on the frontiers of thought. He could explain a theory beautifully, but he could never fashion one. Others might complain that he was so serene that he could never express poetic emotions. The anguish of unrequited love, the bitterness of despair, the exhilaration of unexpected triumph, not even the ecstasy of religious fulfillment were his to experience and to express. Even lacking these qualities he would have had a stronger impact upon the critical reader if he could have condensed better. He seemed to have recognized this defect and occasionally wrote compendia of longer works. These compendia, however, could not capture the desired concentration of the message without some tendency to a blandness from which the longer works largely escaped.

Fray Luis de Granada has captured an important place in the history of Spanish religious literature. His works are still printed today, more for individual devotion than for scholarly analysis. His serenity, which was his religious strength, was perhaps his literary limitation, but his valuable contributions to religious literature should be cherished.

Notes and References

Chapter One

1. The high points of the Catholic-Lutheran confrontation were: Luther's call for reform; his Ninety-five Theses posted at Wittenberg University on October 31, 1517; his unsuccessful defense before the Emperor Charles V and the Diet of Worms in 1521; the failure of reconciliation at Augsburg, June 25, 1530; and the confirmation of the irrevocable split at the Ecumenical Council of Trent (1545–1563).

2. Philip Melanchthon (1497–1560) was the most diplomatic of the followers of Luther. He labored unsuccessfully to accommodate the Lutheran reform to Catholic orthodoxy.

3. Desiderius Erasmus (1467–1536), the great Dutch humanist, sought liberal reforms within the orthodox Catholic church. He remained under suspicion of heterodoxy, however, in the minds of conservative religious leaders, especially Spaniards, and many of his followers suffered the punishment of the Inquisition.

4. *Iluminado* and *alumbrado* mean illuminated or enlightened. *Dejado* suggests that the person has abandoned his will to the religious experience and has become passive.

5. The genuineness of some mystical experiences and the falaciousness of apparently similar experiences is of course a vast problem, not germane to our story. We are interested merely in picturing the ambience in which claims and accusations are considered with dire seriousness.

6. Evelyn Underhill, *Mysticism* (New York: E. P. Dutton, 1961), p. 89.

7. An excellent example of this in Spanish literature is the play by Tirso de Molina, *El condenado por desconfiado* (*The Man Condemned for His Lack of Faith*). The protagonist strove for ascetic perfection but had no love in his heart.

Chapter Two

1. Mateo Solana y Gutiérrez, *Fray Luis de Granada* (México: Editora del continente, 1942), p. 11, states that Granada was born the day of Isabella's death (November 25).

The biographical notes are taken from several sources. The central one is Fray Justo Cuervo, *Biografía de Fray Luis de Granada* (Madrid: Librería de Gregorio del Amo, 1895). Additional notes of value are in the introduction to Luis de Granada, *Obras*, Biblioteca de autores españoles, vol. VI (Madrid: Ediciones Atlas, 1944). The introduction is by Don José Joaquín de Mora. Also Fray Luis de Granada, *Obra selecta*, Biblioteca de autores cristianos (Madrid: Editorial Católica, 1947), with the biographical introduction by Fray Desiderio Diez de Triana. Cuervo is a brilliant scholar, but one must occasionally be on guard against his partisan zeal. He is especially concerned about a polemic he held with the rival Franciscan order's publication *Eco*, which disputes in part Granada's authorship of the *Libro de la oración y meditación*. Cuervo also expressed disdain for de Mora, saying that all he did was copy the good and bad from an eighteenth-century biographer, Luis de Muñoz. De Mora, however, is praised by E. Allison Peers, a noted British authority on Spanish mystics. Diez de Triana has the most interestingly written biography. It too contains an emotional tone and perhaps a slight tendency to romanticize the subject.

2. Cuervo, p. 10.

3. *Biblioteca de autores españoles* VI, xiii: hereafter this will be cited as *BAE*.

4. Cuervo, p. 11.

5. Ibid., p. 13.

6. *BAE*, p. xv.

7. Ibid.

8. Cuervo, pp. 36–45.

9. Ibid., pp. 49–56.

10. Ibid., p. 57

11. Ibid., pp. 82–120.

12. Ibid., p. 14

13. Three Castilian translations prior to Granada's are known: An obscure anonymous translation of 1490 was followed by the translation by Menardo Ungot Alamano y Lanzalao in Sevilla in 1493 and another anonymous translation in 1512. Espasa Calpe, *Enciclopedia universal ilustrada*, LXII, 594–95.

14. Probably the most widely used translation is that of Father Nieremberg in 1658. Fray Luis Getino modernized Granada's version for Aguilar's "Colección crisol" (Madrid, 1951). Like his predecessor Cuervo, Getino argues for Granada against a rival, claiming that Nieremberg had only modernized Granada's translation.

15. The biographers seem to agree that he wrote the *Libro de la oración y meditación* while at Scala Coeli. This could have meant that it was completed a good many years before its publication. He may not even have thought of publishing it when he first wrote it.

16. *Biblioteca de autores cristianos*, xxxvii-xl.

17. Fray Justo Cuervo, *Fray Luis de Granada y la Inquisición* in (*Homenaje a Menéndez Pelayo* Madrid 1899).

18. Quietism, a passive, semimystical state was regarded as heretical during this period. It became a controversial phenomenon in the seventeenth century with the work of Molinos.

19. Cuervo, *Biografía*, p. 42.

20. Ibid., pp. 23–24.

21. *Biblioteca de autores cristianos.*

22. Cuervo, p. 163, quotes Granada as saying that all his other works are taken from these. This was before he wrote the *Introducción del símbolo de la fe.*

23. *BAE*, Vol. XI, pp. 1–57, 493–642, 194.

24. E. Allison Peers, *Studies of the Spanish Mystics* (London: Macmillan, 1951), p. 30.

25. Cuervo, p. 137.

26. Ibid., p. 153.

Chapter Three

1. The standard bibliography of Granada's works is Máximo Llaneza, *Bibliografía del V. P. M. Fray Luis de Granada*, 4 vols. (Salamanca: Establecimiento typográfico de Calatrava, 1926–1928). Llaneza's bibliography is almost entirely concerned with editions of Granada's works.

2. An isolated but significant exception to this statement is the edition of the *Guía de pecadores* in the series Clásicos castellanos (Madrid: Espasa Calpe, 1942). In the introduction Matías Martínez Burgos explains that the first edition was chosen and only the first two books were used. Thus the work has only two hundred and forty-six pages of text. He seemed to have preferred this arrangement to the alternative which would perhaps have run to four volumes.

3. Bataillon, Marcel, *Erasmo y España* (Traducción de Antonio Alatorre), II, 196–207, and Alonso, Dámaso, *De los siglos oscuros al de oro* (Madrid: Ed. Gredos, 1964, pp. 218–225.

4. Sileni are small images resembling satyrs. Their repulsive exterior reminded Plato of Socrates who was physically unattractive but who had great worth as the sileni did for those who used them in religious rites.

5. *BAE*, VI, 79. Incidentally those who follow the *Guía de Pecadores* in this volume have one unusual source of confusion. There is no chapter marked XIII; Chapters XIV through XXIV in Part II should have been numbered XIII through XXIII respectively. Likewise Part III should have the Chapters XXIV–XXIX instead of XXV–XXX. I checked with another edition of the *Guía de Pecadores* (Aguilar's *Colección crisol*) to be reassured that nothing was omitted from the *BAE* text, simply the number was skipped.

6. Ibid., p. 83.

7. The reference naturally recalls *La vida es sueño* (*Life Is a Dream*) by Calderón, but the two authors are not very similar. Granada sees the unreality of a dream in this mortal life since it passes so quickly, while Calderón sees it as unreal because truths are so hard to distinguish from illusions.

8. Cervantes reinforces this point in *Don Quijote*, Part II, Chapter VIII: "All vices, Sancho, bring a kind of pleasure with them except for envy which brings only disappointments, rancors, and rages."

9. *BAE*, VI, 142.

10. Granada adds, as an appendix to the *Sinner's Guide*, a "Letter from Bishop Eucherius to Valerian" translated by Fray Juan de la Cruz, a man who died before the publication of *Sinner's Guide*. Eucherius was bishop of Lyons (432–441). Granada introduces him as a student of St. Augustine. Since neither the original nor its translation is by Granada, and since the appendix really adds little to our understanding of *Sinner's Guide*, I will not comment further upon it.

Chapter Four

1. *BAE*, VIII, 59. The date of volume VIII is 1945.

2. Ibid., p. 61

3. Ibid., p. 75.

4. Ibid., p. 81.

5. St. Theresa has essentially the same idea. She says that oral prayer is not prayer at all unless accompanied by meditation. *Moradas* (Chapter I).

6. St. Theresa's analogy briefly is that mystic union is a cooperative effort of God and the soul. The soul gradually does less and God more until the soul becomes completely passive and God does it all. With the water analogy she mentions four stages: the water may be obtained by a well, by a water wheel, by irrigation from a stream, or by rain (see Chapter XI of her *Life*).

7. *BAE*, VIII, 184

8. Ibid., p. 352

9. Others express the illuminative and purgative ways with more stages: prayer of quiet, prayer of union or betrothal, dark night of the soul, and the spiritual marriage. Professor Hatzfeld adds a still higher one for St. John of the Cross: the "living flame of love."

10. *BAE*, VIII, 416

11. Ibid., p. 423.

12. Ibid., p. 377.

13. Ibid., p. 378.

14. Ibid.

15. Ibid., p. 382.

16. Ibid., p. 383.

17. For example, see Underhill, p. 268.

18. *BAE*, VIII, 393.

19. Ibid., p. 422.

20. Ibid., p. 426.

Chapter Five

1. According to Granada grace can lift men above the status of angels. *BAE*, VI, 204.

2. For those who wish to examine a complete catalog of Granada's references to nature, there is the study by Sister Mary Bernarda Brentano, *Nature in the Works of Fray Luis de Granada* (Washington: Catholic University Press, 1936). This work gives Granada's references to nature, first inorganic nature, from the heavenly bodies to the basic four elements and next organic nature, the plants and the animals, first domestic, then wild. Many of the references are to understanding nature itself. Many others, especially those not taken from the *Introduction to the Symbol of Faith*, are intended to present analogies from nature to provide guidance to man in his everyday conduct. The sister's scholarship is careful, her interpretations cautious.

3. I assume that Fray Luis at this point was thinking how easily air carries moisture up with it. He was not thinking of the bubbles one might observe upon seeing air escape from under a pool of water.

4. There is no discussion here of the element fire. It is possibly an oversight on Granada's part; possibly he concluded that so little is known of the region of fire that he felt that he could not comment usefully.

5. Brentano, p. 152.

6. *BAE*, VI, 372.

7. Ibid., p. 521.

8. Ibid., p. 527.

9. Ibid., p. 564.

10. Ibid., p. 654.

11. Ibid., p. 658.

12. Ibid., p. 615.

13. Ibid., p. 623.

14. Ibid., p. 630.

15. Ibid., p. 651.

16. Ibid., p. 703.

17. Ibid., p. 712.

Chapter Six

1. *BAE*, XI, 443. The date of this volume is 1945.

2. Ibid., p. 469.

3. *De Imitatione Christi* (Taurini: Marii e. Marietti, 1927). Incidentally, the editor of this edition does not accept Thomas à Kempis as the author.

4. Madrid: Aguilar, 1951.

5. *BAE*, XI, 299.

6. Ibid., p. 329.
7. Ibid., p. 333.
8. Ibid., pp. 1–57.
9. Ibid., p. 28.
10. New York: Instituto de las Españas en los Estados Unidos, 1927.

Chapter Seven

1. Fray Luis de Granada, *Obras,* Edición crítica y completa por Father Justo Cuervo, 14 vols. (Madrid: Viuda e hija de G. Fuentenebro, 1906–1908).
2. Justo Cuervo, *Biografía de Fray Luis de Granada* (Madrid: Librería de Gregorio del Amo, 1895).
3. Justo Cuervo, "Fray Luis de Granada y la Inquisición," in *Homenaje a Menéndez Pelayo* (Madrid, 1899).
4. E. Allison Peers, *Studies of the Spanish Mystics* (London: Sheldon Press, 1930), II, 108–11.
5. Máximo Llaneza, *Bibliografía del V. P. M. Fray Luis de Granada,* (Salamanca, 1926–1928).
6. Collección Crisol (Madrid: Aguilar, 1951).
7. Ibid.
8. Spanish version preceded by an introduction by Pedro Umbert (Barcelona: Imprenta de Henrich y Compañía, 1907).
9. For Volume I, I am using the revised edition (New York: Macmillan, 1951). See also note 4.
10. Marcel Bataillon, *Erasmo y España,* trans. Antonio Alatorre (Mexico: Fondo de Cultura Económica, 1950).
11. Rousselot, p. 185.
12. Ibid., p. 212.
13. Peers, I, 39.
14. Ibid., pp. 35–36; the translator is Peers.
15. Ibid., p. 61.
16. *Revue de Littérature comparée* XVI (January–March, 1936), 23–39.
17. Bataillon points out with some feeling that Cano, whom he describes as a "super sleuth", found this passage by Granada objectionable, but did not recognize it as Savonarola's (Ibid., p. 33).
18. A statement from Granada more in keeping with his general philosophy is found in the *Memorial of the Christian Life* Treatise V, Chapter IV: "Vocal prayer is very helpful for all people especially for beginners"; and he adds the caveat, "if it is done with desirable attention and devotion" (*BAE,* VIII, 304).
19. *Revue,* pp. 30–31.
20. *De los siglos oscuros al de oro* (Madrid: Editorial Gredos, 1964), pp. 218–25.
21. Ibid., pp. 221–23.

22. "Los místicos del norte y Fray Luis de Granada," *Archivo Ibero-Americano* 7, no. 25 (January–March, 1947), 5–29; 7, nos. 26–28 (April–December, 1947), 145–65.

23. Suso translated Tauler's works into Latin along with works by some of Tauler's students without distinguishing the master's from the students' contributions. Fidel de Ros gives this title to the author of a work called *Exercita super vita et passione salvatoris*. Therefore there may be more than one Pseudo Tauler.

24. The work of Herp that Fidel de Ros cites is *Directorium aureum* (see Ros, p. 159).

25. José Martínez Ruiz (Azorín), *Los dos Luises y otros ensayos* (Buenos Aires: Espasa Calpe, Colección Austral, 1944).

26. Ibid., pp. 53–54.

27. José Martínez Ruiz (Azorín), *De Granada a Castelar* (Madrid: R. Caro Reggio, 1922).

Chapter Eight

1. There are more than one hundred names cited plus many others identified only as "a doctor." It is not possible to divide these into ascetic and spiritual, theological and pious, or any other such pairing since a number of the writers such as St. Augustine and St. Bernard seem to be on Granada's mind for any explanation or inspiration. He tries to find good in all writers except those whom he considers extollers of the flesh: the Epicureans and the Mohammedans, and the *Talmud*, which he finds thoroughly confusing.

2. Defined by Webster's *New Collegiate Dictionary* as "Remission of part or all of the temporal and especially purgatorial punishment that according to Roman Catholicism is due for sins whose eternal punishment has been remitted and whose guilt has been pardoned (as through the sacrament of penance)." In the popular mind indulgences were statements that a person had been forgiven for sins by payment of a gift to the church. The need for the accompanying contrition is often overlooked.

3. *BAE*, VI, 219.

Selected Bibliography

PRIMARY SOURCES

Because many editions of unequal quality and varying accessibility exist, only the most useful or readily obtainable have been included here, with indications to guide the reader.

1. Collected Editions

GRANADA, FRAY LUIS DE. *Obras* 14 vols, ed. Fray Justo Cuervo (Madrid: viuda e hija de G. Fuentenebro, 1906–8). This scholarly edition, in mercifully large print, is the best one from which to work though not the most accessible.

————. in *Biblioteca de autores españoles* Vols. VI, VIII, and XI. Recent printings list it as Vols. I, II, and III of the works of Granada. (Madrid: Atlas, 1944). The print is small and occasionally some lines are blurred, but since most libraries have it, the reader can readily follow the notes.

————. *Obra selecta* (Madrid: Biblioteca de autores cristianos, 1947). An anthology edited to conform to the order of the *Summa Teologica* of St. Thomas Aquinas.

2. Individual Works.

GRANADA, FRAY LUIS DE. *Obras* 14 vols, ed. Fray Justo Cuervo (Madrid: Espasa Calpe, 1942). This edition is taken from the first edition, 1556, not the more common revised edition of 1567.

————. *Guía de pecadores* Colección crisol (Madrid: Aguilar, 1945).

3. Translations by Granada

KEMPIS, TOMASA. *Imitación de Cristo.* Translated by Fray Luis de Granada. Colección crisol, (Madrid: Aguilar, 1951).

SECONDARY SOURCES

1. Books

ALONSO, DAMASO. *De los siglos oscuros al de oro.* (Madrid: Editorial Gredos, 1964). Includes short article on Erasmus and Granada.

BATAILLON, MARCEL. *Erasmo y España* Translated by Antonio Alatorre. 2 vols. (México: fondo de Cultura Económica, 1950). A definitive study

157

of religious controversy in the one hundred years following Erasmus. Granada figures prominently.

BRENTANO, MARY BERNARDA. *Nature in the Works of Fray Luis de Granada.* (Washington: Catholic University Press, 1936). A careful, thorough study.

CUERVO, JUSTO. *Biografía de Fray Luis de Granada.* (Madrid: Librería de Gregorio del Amo, 1895). The best biography. Attached to it is his study *Fray Luis de Granada, verdadero y único autor del "Libro de la oración."*

LLANEZA, MAXIMO. *Bibliografía del V. P. M. Fray Luis de Granada* 4 vols. (Salamanca, Establecimiento typográfico de Calatrava, 1926–1928. This study needs to be brought up to date and critical studies on Granada added.

MARTÍNEZ RUIZ, JOSÉ. (AZORÍN). *De Granada a Castelar.* Madrid: R. Caro Reggio, 1922. A treatise on eloquence in which Granada is stressed.

————. *Los dos Luises y otros ensayos.* Colección Austral. Buenos Aires: Espasa Calpe, 1944. A large section devoted to a series of vignettes about Granada.

PEERS, EDGAR ALLISON. *Studies of the Spanish Mystics.* Vol. 1. Rev. ed. London: S.P.C.K., 1951. Vol. 2. London: Sheldon Press, 1930. Granada viewed in the perspective of other mystics.

ROUSSELOT, PAUL. *Los místicos españoles.* Translated by Pedro Umbert. Barcelona: Imprenta de Henrich y Compañía, 1907. A significant early study.

SWITZER, REBECCA. *The Ciceronian Style in Fray Luis de Granada.* New York: Instituto de las Españas en los Estados Unidos, 1927. (The definitive work in its field.)

UNDERHILL, EVELYN. *Mysticism.* New York: E. P. Dutton, 1961. An excellent introduction to mysticism. Significance for Granada studies is only indirect.

2. Articles

BATAILLON, MARCEL. "De Savonarole à Louis de Granade." *Revue de Littérature comparée* Vol. 16 (January–March, 1936), 23–39.

CUERVO, JUSTO. "Fray Luis de Granada y la Inquisición." In *Homenaje a Menéndez Pelayo.* Madrid: V. Suárez, 1899. Vol. I, pp. 733–743.

MOORE, JOHN A. "A Note on Erasmus and Granada" *Romance Notes* 9, no. 2 (1968), 314–19. My own reaction to the views of Bataillon and Alonso.

ROS, FIDEL DE. "Los místicos del norte y Fray Luis de Granada." *Archivo Iberoamericano* 7, no. 25 (January–March, 1947), 5–29; 7, nos. 26–28 (April–December, 1947), 145–65. A further study into Granada's sources.

Index